Trout Madness by John D. Voelker
(aka Robert Traver)
inspired me to spend more time fishing for
trout, and less time on what society perceives as
important, most everything else.

I never acquired his expertise as a trout
fisherman, or as an author, but his words have
pushed me to endless hours trying.

For that, I am ever thankful.

Bob O'Brien

The Trout Fishermen: Bonding Waters

Bob O'Brien
and
Darin Rauguth

The Trout Fishermen:
Bonding Waters
Copyright © 2016
Bob O'Brien - Darin Rauguth

Comments: prosencons@live.com

Paper Back
ISBN: 978-1-941069-56-1
Hard cover
ISBN: 978-1-941069-60-8

Cover Picture: Fran O'Brien

Illustrations: Bob O'Brien

Prose Press
Pawleys Island, SC
prosencons@live.com

ACKNOWLEDGEMENTS

Thanks to our wives, Fran and Lisa, and the encouragers as well as kibitzers who took an interest in our little collection of stories.

A special thanks to my friends
Linda Ketron and Barry Kelly
for their advice and direction.

*"I suspect that men are going this way
for the last time, and
I for one don't want to waste the trip."*

*John D. Voelker pen name,
Robert Traver*

CONTENTS

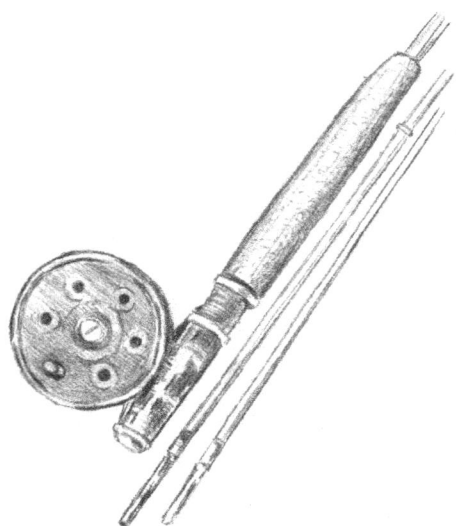

The Bamboo Rod

I was about twelve when I became intrigued with trout fishing. Maybe I read about it in one of the sportsman's magazines, *Outdoor Life* or *Field & Stream*, I don't recall. It looked like the ultimate challenge where a person would need skill, patience and a knowledge of nature to succeed. My first rod, that was something really special.

The wooden box was marked "Calcutta cane," but I don't remember a brand name. Inside a soft cloth sleeve protected a split bamboo fly rod that came with two tips. One was a little stiffer than the other and both leaned a little to the left. I acquired this treasure by cashing in two books of Gold Bond stamps. In the late 1940s, saving stamps were handed out by local merchants as an incentive to keep loyal customers loyal.

Most of today's rods are fiberglass and graphite. They are light, strong, cast effortlessly and are way overpriced. Split bamboo rods are a little heaver in weight and price – running in the thousands. I'd be happy with that old "Calcutta cane" magic stick today, if it were the only rod I ever owned, and it would never be valued in dollars.

The Prairie River

Spring: Snow becomes a few drops of water trickling down into valleys, joining raging streams, seeking to become part of the great sea.

Ruby Sue Tootser

" *Real men love the rustic life in God's country.*" That beer bottle bull-crap was just one of the many falsehoods preached to teenaged boys growing up in 1950 Wisconsin. Being the gullible macho follower I was in those days, I believed their spiel. It was undoubtedly the main reason I quit a perfectly good, but boring government job, in Waukesha, Wisconsin and dragged my wife and two daughters 150 miles north to Merrill, Wisconsin, just south of Tomahawk. God's country.

I was hired by a poorly run little printing company whose owners viewed employees as semi-slaves, beholden to the company store, and like the plantation owners of yesteryear, the company was close to being the only game in town.

Not being the submissive type, I only lasted a little

over a year before they canned me, but that's another story.

I have always been over infatuated with fishing for Trout. I suspect it may have been self-induced brainwashing based on the half true tales of challenging conquests spun by descriptive writers and an overdose of wishful thinking. Standing in a Trout stream freezing my butt off seemed so important when I was in my twenties.

For me, the self-serving jerk I was in those days (still am all too often), it was a happy day when we arrived in Merrill; for my wife and kids, not so much. When it only warmed up to four above zero, day or night, in January, I began to realize it was too damn cold in Merrill, Wisconsin to do much of anything. Winter was long, summer short, and spring was the first day above freezing. The snow melted a few weeks before the season opened, the first Saturday in May. I'd waited all winter. I was raring to go.

Sully's Bar was my one bright spot in the sea of depression called Merrill. "Hey, the city boy," Sully would say to no one in particular when I walked in. Sully's was a typical Wisconsin watering hole; a massive over-varnished dark wooden bar complete with a brass foot rail, neglected dingy stained oak floor with a stale musty smell that had to have taken years to create. Cheap booze bottles were displayed on the mirrored back bar, and oversized fish and deer peered down from smoke-stained walls.

The cliental fit into Wisconsin's two standard categories, the ever-present hollow-eyed boozers slumped over, drooling in their drinks hours on end and the after-work, high testosterone hunter, fisherman, sports-talking Packer-backers, few of which had ever been to an actual game. Unfortunately, I fit the mold; still do.

A frosty schooner of Shlitz, Sully's signature drink, is still my all time favorite. After downing a couple, I felt like one of Sully's regulars. The Friday after-work crowd were mostly local native beer drinking, "BS" fishermen. That included their leader, Sully himself. A week before opening day, they shared one of their secret spots with me; a secluded stretch of the Prairie River that could only be accessed using a Sully-friendly farmer's private road.

I arrived an hour before dawn along with about 100 other eager anglers who apparently shared the secret spot. A radiant star-filled sky produced just enough light to let me find my stuff – waders, new graphite fly rod, basket creel, lucky hat, gloves, and my canvas hunting jacket with pockets already filled with extra everything, and more flies than I'd use in two lifetimes. Every fisherman suiting up had to be colder than a witch's . . .

Patches of snow, unrelenting to spring, were still scattered throughout the woods. As I ambled down a mucky path to the stream, I could feel my heartbeat race and face flush as my anticipation level peaked. When I reached the water, I was taken aback by the level. An inch higher and she'd have been over her banks.

A guy, dressed a lot like me in rubber and canvas, was

standing a little upstream looking over the water. "Pretty high," I said as I approached him.

"Not bad," he said, "a hell of a lot better than last year."

"I'm a first-timer here,"

"It's a tough stream," he said sarcastically, frowning at me as if to say, *Just what we need another a-hole city boy screwing up the stream.*

I passed him quickly thinking, *know-it-all jerk.*

Yankee Rapids, the spot I was heading for, was far enough upstream that I passed most of the "opening-day-only-crowd" along the way. I heard the rapids before I saw them. Beautiful intimidating water thundered over the boulders and raced helter-skelter through deep pools. *Wow,* I thought, *I'm too much of a candy-ass to wade into that torrent.*

The path had vanished a half a mile back downstream. I walked, crawled over, around, and through, the brush, downed trees, and boulders along the bank, cautiously searching a spot where I might ease in. When I finally did get in the water, I realized I had underestimated the current's force. Even the shallow water was deeper than it looked. Moving very slowly, struggling to just stay vertical, I managed to send a few wet flies to the top of several runs and into couple pools.

After three hours of freezing my butt off without a hint of a trout, I crawled out, popped open a can of Schlitz, and began to second guess my decision to move to "God's Country." Hell, I doubt God would live there.

The headwaters of Yankee Rapids was not quite as intimidating as the rapids, but I was still anxious about the fast water and slippery stones. I thought to myself, *You can do this. You can do this,* until I found myself waist-deep, inching my way to a spot parallel to and slightly below where I wanted to place my fly.

After flogging the air until my line was extended, my little streamer splashed the water like a rock. *Nice shot A-hole,* I cursed my fatigue and lack of patience and stripped the line quickly trying to take up the slack in the rushing water. Without feeling the hit, I saw my line heading upstream. My first thought, *Damn I'm caught on a log or something. No, the bottom's moving.* My new fiberglass rod began to pump. *Stay on, baby, you little prick.* I didn't take enough time to play the fish, enjoy his maneuvers, or give him the respect he deserved. I managed to horse him into the net, but I knew a bigger fish would have been long gone.

By the time I dragged my sorry ass back to my car, it was after 3:00. *Funny,* I thought, walking back along the stream, *everybody's gone; wonder where?* Maybe I wasn't the only one demoralized by the Prairie River on that cold and dreary Spring day.

"How'd ya do?" Sully, the unofficial leader of the BS fishermen and owner of Sully's Bar, asked, as I slurped the foam from my giant schooner of Schlitz.

"One thirteen-inch Brown," I said truthfully. "And

three sisters a little smaller," I said after seeing his smirk.

"A lot of guys out there?" he asked with his head down, his eyes peaking out from under the lids.

"Not many," I said knowing full well he knew it was a circus out there.

"How'd they do?"

"Great from what I could tell from the look of their creels," I said. "How did you do?"

He went to the freezer inside his cooler and brought out four of the biggest Brook Trout I'd ever seen.

They looked to be about 14 inches – minimum, solid, stocky fish, with strong vibrant color that signaled truly native Trout. As hard as I tried to hide my reaction, I'm sure Sully saw my green-eyed amazement. "Those are really nice, Sully."

"We ate the small ones," he said sheepishly.

I fished the Prairie off-and-on most of that summer. Did pretty well too, once the water dropped, but I was reluctant to hike up to Yankee Rapids again, it was always seemed a bit too far.

The Sully-schooner never tasted quite as good after that opening weekend, and Sully and his buddies, the guys, well, they became small fish in a small pond in my eyes.

And . . . small fish have never been much of an attraction.

Yankee Rapids

Northern Wisconsin's bitter cold winter is soon forgotten as sunny days and the fresh smell of pine on a cool breeze invigorate those hardy enough to take advantage of the natural beauty.

Once summer arrived, I abandoned my wife and kids more often than I should have. My "call of the wild" was to explore most of the trout streams in the area – some good, some not so good. As I moved from one exciting new stretch of water to the next, I kept thinking about the water that had beaten me so badly on opening day. As unrewarding as my experience was at Yankee Rapids, I thought low water in August should present a better outcome.

I pulled off the road at first light and, once again, parked in the farmer's field. Three deer grazing at the far side of the field looked up but didn't scamper off. I guess I wasn't much of a threat. Untrampled grass told me no one had been here for quite some time. *That's a good sign,*

I thought, and I always believed seeing deer was a good omen.

I was surprised at my enthusiasm as I worked my way along the stream. The path was grown over, *another good sign*, but it meant walking around, over, under, and through brush, and more obstacles along the way. I was hot and sweating in spite of choosing to fish in jeans and old sneakers instead of waders. But – I wore my canvas jacket, which didn't help. It was either that or get all scratched up. When I got to Yankee Rapids, the water seemed to be running with the same power it had on opening day – thank God there was only half as much of it.

The first promising spot was at the bottom of the rapids. Water spilled over and between several boulders forming a pool that I'd missed in the Spring. Without getting too close, I could see it was deep, very deep. It looked good to me.

"Here we go," I whispered, *"slowdown, take your time."* I attached a "Muddler Minnow" fly that I liked to use whenever grasshoppers were in season. I eased into the water and moved far enough out from the bank to have room to back cast. *Cold, damn it's cold,* I wished I'd worn my waders.

On the first cast my fly landed softly, about eight feet above the hole on my side of the stream. I stripped line fast keeping up with the current while simultaneously moving the fly to the edge the deeper water. I saw a golden flash as my line went taut. *Brown,* I thought, *decent size.* He headed upstream straining my rod with authority. Just when I thought everything was under control, he turned and headed in my direction faster than I could strip line. As he darted two feet from my legs, I realized he was waving good-by. I imagined seeing a smirk on his face as he passed me. *You win this time, but I'll be back.*

I eased out of the stream and quietly skirted the hole, planning to visit it on my way back. Yankee Rapids, the once-raging torrent, had become a series of plateaus separated by powerful runs over a bottom made up of slippery rocks and submerged boulders. The current was swift by non-mountain standards, but for a stream in the Midwest, it couldn't be better.

I reentered the stream at a flat stretch about twenty-five yards upstream from where I'd just lost the Brown. The current was faster than it looked. I moved cautiously to a narrow island in the middle of the stream, crawled out, and stood for a moment surveying the water. The sun was about nine o'clock high. *Feels good,* I thought, beginning to warm up.

I meticulously fished runs on both sides of the island without success. I thought there'd be a hungry fish on at least one of the sides. Wrong again. When I ran out of island, about forty yards upstream, I reluctantly slid back into the frigid water.

An oval pool below boulders along the east bank was

dark in the morning shade. *If I were a Brown, that's where I'd hangout.* I reveled in my brilliance when an under-sized Brown grabbed the fly on my third cast. "Is your daddy out there?" I said, gently putting him back in the water. Apparently he was an orphan, or his daddy wasn't fooled by me.

For the next two hours I fished that beautiful stretch of water, Yankee Rapids, with persistence and to the best of my ability, changing from the Muddler, to streamers, nymphs, wet, and dry flies. It was after eleven. Frustration was setting in. *One more hour*, I thought, *max.*

I moved toward a spot, where I thought it would be easy to fish a run ending in a pool on the far side of the stream. Getting there proved to be harder than I'd figured. Powerful current held me in place as I reached a gap between a boulder and an old log. Holding the stubby branch on the log, I tried to pull forward. "Shit," I shouted, when it broke off. It felt like I was in slow motion falling backwards into the current. I held my rod high, tumbled once, twice, three times, maybe more, I'm not sure. I came to a stop and managed to get on my hands and knees. I stayed there for a minute trying to catch my breath. My rod was still intact. The handle of my net became a cane giving me leverage to help me get to my feet.

God must have been watching over me when I chose jeans over waders. In boots, I'd still be rolling down that stream.

It was a long walk back to my car. I was wet, cold, scratched, and bruised – but not broken.

Yankee Rapids, two – not so expert fisherman, zero.

There are many lessons to be learned
fishing for trout.
Humility is surely at the top of the list.

The Wild Rose

The quietness of the night only added to my melancholy. My friend Brad and I were heading along the county blacktop as we had so many Saturdays before. In the predawn sky, twinkling stars were sending me the same coded message over and over again. "This is the last time. You will never get to do this again. This is the last. . ."

I called her The Wild Rose, or sometimes just The Rose, because her headwaters were close to Wild Rose, Wisconsin. I would never tell you, or anyone, for that matter, exactly where that spot is, but I will tell you this: Rose's cold-water sprngs are hidden in a scrub-brush meadow where trickles of water blend together, giving her renewed birth with every sunrise. Some uncreative cartographer, with absolutely no conception of the stream's challenges and without input from me, thought "Willow Creek" was a more appropriate name. But she'll always be The Wild Rose to me.

The Rose, like most of the women in my life, could

be elusive, unpredictable, and temperamental, but if you approached her with patience, always moving slowly and with forethought, she could, on rare occasions, be convinced to give up her treasures.

A hint of light emerged in the east as we approached the field where we always parked. When I turned off the narrow dirt lane, dust followed my old pick-up into the brush.

Brad quickly cranked up his window. "Damn," he said. "We need rain in the worst way. I hope the creek has enough water to fish. Maybe we should just go get breakfast."

"Not a chance, Brad. I sure as hell didn't drag my butt out of bed in the middle of the night for eggs."

Brad smiled his impish smirk, and I realized he was pulling my chain. "You gonna sit here and babble or are we goin' fishin'?"

"All right then – It's time."

We lumbered out of the truck, dropped the back gate, pumped and lit the Coleman, and slapped some of the dust off our paraphernalia.

I fished The Rose in jeans, a pair of old tennis shoes, a khaki hat, and for brush protection, a canvas hunting jacket that usually got too warm by mid-morning. Brad wore a long-sleeved shirt and over-patched waders that, I was pretty sure, still leaked.

We fished at first light because I had it in my head that

worthy trout "spooked" easily once the sun was high in the sky. My self-proclaimed axiom, *the brighter the day the poorer the fishing,* was especially true on The Rose. Most fishermen seldom fished the late summer's low water, but Brad and I were never part of the "most fishermen" crowd.

Although we each carried a box of flies (wet, dry, nymphs, and a few small streamers), the bait we actually needed to catch fish – worms, crickets, grasshoppers and grubs – was packed in our wicker creels. All of those were personally dug up, trapped, or caught by one of us– probably me.

I don't remember why, but I always gave Brad the choice. "What's it gonna be – upstream or down?"

"I'll go downstream this time," he said with a coy glint. I knew he'd choose downstream. The week before, I managed to fool three nice trout downstream, while upstream, he only caught a barely legal single. The fact that I'd been fishing for these critters most of my life and this was only his second year, mattered little to his competitive nature.

Brad Jones was an art director in a small advertising agency. He became my trout fishing protégée, much to his wife's chagrin, after years of feeding me freelance artwork whenever his company needed an overnight layout. The challenge, and of course greed, motivated me to do whatever it took to show up the next morning with sketches in hand. I had fished alone most of my life until, one weekend when his wife and kids were off on some excursion, he asked to go along. It was nice to have a fishing buddy.

Before we parted, thunder rumbled in the west. "Is that what I think it is?" I asked, turning toward the sound.

"Yup, better take my poncho," Brad replied with a grin, knowing damn well that I never bothered to bring one. "Looks like a front's moving in." He pointed to a huge cloud bank that severed the morning sky.

I love fishing on rainy days; no shadows, my sounds are muffled, and fish venture out to feed on the new food supply washing into the stream. "I'll meet you back here about ten."

Brad gave me a little wave, pointed his rod forward, and like a lancer, charged off to do battle.

Plowing my way through nasty brush, I twisted, turned, zigged and zagged, until I reached the narrow path that led to the center of the first upstream hole. It was a hairpin turn where the current dug deep into the bank running under the spot where I knelt. I tried to be totally still for as long as my patience allowed, hoping the trout wouldn't notice I was on their roof. Ironically, while I was trying not to make a sound, the distant thunder was now closing in, booming all around me.

After flogging the water for ten fruitless minutes, I moved on to the next bend, which was one of my favorite spots. I got in position, close enough to flip a nymph-fly into its headwaters.

Crack. Whoa, I jumped back; lightning was dancing overhead.

Crack. The storm had arrived and there was nowhere to hide.

Crack . . . Crack. *"God, can you back off a tad,"* I whispered. He didn't. The rain started with a few big drops, then a few more, then He opened the floodgates and unleashed the wind. *Too much of a good thing,* I thought.

Apparently the lightning and thunder didn't bother the trout; a nice Brown took the fly after I bounced it deep into the hole. The trout tried to raise a ruckus, but I managed to nudge him to me and hoisted him onto the bank. On narrow overgrown creeks like the Rose, a net is virtually useless. To compensate, my leader was six-pound test; strong enough to hold most fish, weak enough to break when you got hung up on the ever-present roots, an integral part of the trout's lair.

With a trout in hand, I was content knowing I wasn't going to be skunked on my last day. I couldn't imagine the fish's brothers and sisters being dumb enough to make the same mistake so I moved on.

As I made my way to the next hole, water dripped from my hat to my nose and rolled down to my mouth. Even my underwear was soaked. Freezing cold water numbed my ankles when I gingerly stepped through the ripples to the grassy side. After a short walk I got on my hands and knees and crawled to the spot I thought would be most advantageous.

Ever so slowly, I dropped a weighted nymph-fly into the headwater of the hole. As it ran with the current, I anticipated the strike that was sure to come . . . it didn't. I repeated the exercise several times . . . the strike never came. Perhaps my little yarn and foil fly wasn't all that convincing.

I moved from one familiar spot to the next, all the while appreciating the stream's rugged, yet graceful, idiosyncrasies. Rose's straightaways concealed a brisk current that could be felt on your legs more easily than seen. She was like a slalom ski course, twisting and turning, weaving back and forth, digging deep under the bank at every turn. It was the bends, those pockets of protection, that the elusive Brooks and Browns called home. Year after year – I have no idea how many – I spent most Saturday mornings fishing The Rose. I watched her change from season to season, week to week, as God continually refined His masterpiece. My challenge was to recognize and adjust to the changes, evaluate exactly where the trout were, and present a bait as naturally as I could. Sounds easy . . . it never has been.

My grand finale romancing The Wild Rose – five hours passed too quickly. The cold rain showed no sign of letting up, the run-off water turned the creek cloudy, and my clothes were drenched. I had managed to pick up a second Brown, and I considered it a good day. Prolonging the end, I decided to fish one more hole before heading to the truck.

When I arrived at the edge of this final bend, I picked up an earthworm about to fall into the stream. He wiggled on my hook as I tossed him toward a little swirl at the front of the hole. Bam! A hard strike the moment the worm hit the surface. He was beautiful! Over a foot long, solid, and almost totally black from living far under the bank where the sun never shines.

When I got to the truck, Brad was grinning through the window. A "How'd ya do?" raced off his tongue.

"I picked up two early, and a real nice one on the way in." Knowing he couldn't stand to wait another second, I said, "Okay. Let's see what's in your creel."

He lifted the lid displaying four gorgeous trout, two of which were bigger than the one I considered real nice. "At 9 o'clock, I thought I was gonna get to go home whooped again," he said with a Teddy Roosevelt smile, "then all hell broke loose."

"You caught all four in the last hour, in the murky water?"

"Yup. Used worms with this." He held up a little silver spinner I'd given to him when he first started fishing with me. I remembered telling him it might work in cloudy water – I guess it did. Or, more likely, fish were apparently venturing out from beneath the banks to feast on the abundance of food washing into the creek.

"How wet are you?" I asked, noticing the rain had backed off to a drizzle.

"I take it you're not ready to throw in the towel?" Brad said, already knowing the answer.

"I'd hate listening to you tell everybody at the agency how you out-fished me."

"I'll give you an hour and a half," Brad said, "just so you can save your reputation. Any longer than that and my wife will be all over my case."

"Mine too. Up or down?"

His answer surprised me, "I'll go upstream this time; give you a shot at the ones I missed."

Thankful for an extra chance, I went downstream only a short way. I'd rather fish than walk, and this way I'd finish up close to the truck. In the hour that followed, The Rose dropped her protective shields just far enough to allow me the illusion that I was clever enough to fool a few of her precious occupants.

Once I pushed through the brush to the first bend, I used the tip of my rod to flip a limp earthworm into a swirl at the front of the hole. Hit – right at the surface – missed it. Trout, by their very nature, are too leery to be fooled twice, but out of desperation, I put what was left of my worm back in the spot where I originally cast. He must have been some hungry fish because, much to my surprise, he struck again. This time I was the victor.

As I methodically moved upstream, each bend gave up another trout. I now had seven. The rain stopped as I came to my final hole. It wasn't much of a hole really, just a slight turn with current running under overhanging grass. I'd never caught anything there before.

The worm-clad hook was quickly picked up by the current, then it started moving upstream at a very fast pace. I pulled the line taut and the fish ripped it out of my hand. Having no choice, I jumped in the water, tried to get low enough to get under the alders and follow wherever the trout might lead. My line went slack; he'd turned and was racing right at me. Stripping line as fast as I could, I saw him pass me to the right heading downstream. Eventually, I turned him and he was heading back up. When he got to the grassy area, I hoisted him up on shore. He flipped once and was off the hook, flopping toward the stream. Half in, half out of the creek, I tried to block his path but he jumped to the side. Reaching out to grab him, I managed to touch his back just as he landed in the water. Unfortunately, my momentum sent me tumbling in after him. *Was I really that inept, or was he just superior? Perhaps a little of both.*

As I crawled out on my hands and knees, I saw Brad standing a few feet back watching and shaking his head. "That had to be the Granddaddy of all Granddaddies."

"He sure as hell was a lot more fish than I could handle," I said. "I'm just glad he didn't drown me."

"I can't believe you're smiling," Brad said looking concerned.

"Brad, that was undoubtedly the most fun I've ever

had out here."

"But you just lost the greatest fish this stream will ever see."

"That may be true, but just knowing he is out there is the reason we're willing to get up in the middle of the night and stand shivering in the rain for hours. I'm happy just having had a chance to meet him."

On our walk back to the truck, it didn't take long before Brad asked, "How many did you get?"

"Eight. How about you?"

"Nine," he said, failing to hold back a smile. I couldn't have been happier for him; he'd come a long way in two short seasons.

When I think back on that day, I can't help but wonder; by allowing me to touch her most cherished prize had The Wild Rose been saying, "farewell, my friend," or was it an attempt to lure me into canceling my move to South Carolina.

Many years have passed since that stormy farewell to The Rose. I only seem to fish "fly-only" water now, and I don't eat what I catch anymore. No matter how expert the chef, trout doesn't taste as good to me as the fish that roamed The Rose. God took my friend Brad a few years after I moved away. He was such a good man; I'm sure he got to go upstream. I fish alone now.

I never returned to The Wild Rose; I never will. She couldn't live up to the image I've tucked away in the treasured memories section of my mind.

The Wild Rose – a loved but unconquered mistress. I miss her.

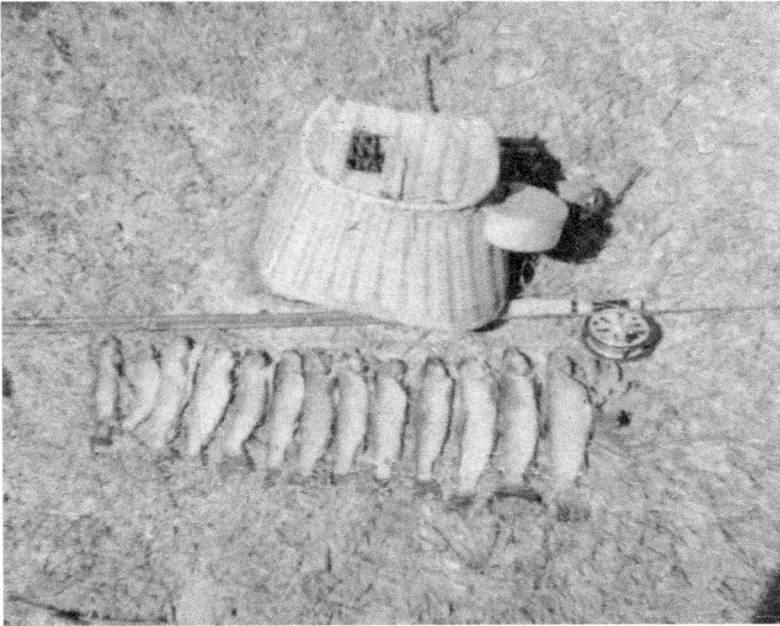

A great day on The Rose
She seldom gave up this many

The Rose – The Teacher
Time with The Wild Rose provided me with insight for most of life's challenges:

It helps to get an early start.
Work is hard, rewards are small, and time is short.
Persistence and patience is no guarantee, but without them failure is assured.
Enjoy loyal friends, they are special.
You travel together, but you fish alone.
Like the wily trout, all God's treasures have been given to us to enjoy.

31

To my friend, Brad Jones

May the road rise up to meet you.
May the wind be always at your back.
May the sun shine warm upon your face;
the rains fall soft upon your fields
and until we meet again,
may God hold you in the palm of His hand.

(gaelic blessing)

The Little Elkhart

When my job in Neenah, Wisconsin, was phased out, (that's a nice way of saying, I was being dumped), I tried to find something, anything, in one of the mountain states. I ended up in Elkhart, Indiana, where the terrain is, as the cliché goes, *flatter than pee on a plate.* Corn fields are even more boring than dairy farms; at least I like cows and milk. Another cliché that influenced my decision to move to Indiana was, *hunger is a great motivator*, and Miles Laboratories was my only job offer.

It took a couple of months after becoming a Hoosier before I met a guy outdoorsy enough to suggest he heard that the Little Elkhart River was supposed to have trout in it. That was a far cry from the type of recommendation I was hoping for but, desperate to find a stream reasonably close to home, I figured, it's worth a look. The second Saturday in August was my first chance to go stream hunting.

A road map took me fifteen miles east to a little Amish town called Middlebury. I didn't learn a thing from the folks in the local breakfast restaurant but the fresh eggs, sausage, and fresh baked bread were fantastic.

The Little Elkhart's headwaters are a couple of narrow, shallow, spring-fed forks southeast of Middlebury. The main trunk of the stream runs right through town then flows northwest to Bristol where it enters the St. Joseph River which eventfully empties into Lake Michigan.

I pulled into the parking lot of a pretty little park at the edge of town. There were swings, monkey bars, a teeter-totter, and picnic tables, all too close to the stream from my viewpoint. *I'm a long way from Wisconsin,* I thought. *Good grief, swings? This is remote?* I slipped into a total depression when I saw a grass barren path at the edge of the water. *How many hundreds of foot steps did it take to wear down the grass to mud? God only knows.*

In spite of my depressed mood, I decided to look over the stream. It was well on its way to being a hot summer day, so I chose to walk into the water wearing beat-up tennis shoes and jeans. I like to do that on hot days. Something told me waders would have been a better choice; I should have listened. The water was a lot colder than I thought it would be. This was my first hint that trout may be able to survive in Indiana.

Day 1

When I explore new water with a mindset to cover a lot of ground, I strap a broken down fly rod to my back and use an ultra light spinning rod with a small Mepps spinner. I like to move upstream at a faster pace than I usually fish, casting the spinner at a 10 or 2 o'clock angle, wherever the stream has potential.

Watermarks on downed logs and the height of the bank above the water told me the stream was at its late summer low. The bottom, primarily sand and pebbles had washed out under downed trees and brush creating the perfect trout lair. At every bend the undercut was deep and dark. *If I were a trout I'd like this selection of hiding places.*

I was unable to quickly cover this woodsy section of this stream. If I wanted to give the water a fair evaluation, I had to crawl over, under, and around downed trees and avoid deep pockets where the water looked iffy. I was out of the water half the time plowing through brush and stinging nettles that had to be at least six foot high. Nettles, for those who may be unfamiliar with them, are nasty, nasty, nasty. They sting like fire for about ten minutes every time they touch bare skin. *I wish I had my jacket and waders on,* I kept thinking, *I wish I had my jacket and my waders on.*

I fished a lot of promising water that morning without a hint of a fish. It was close to 11 and I was totally discouraged, when I saw a small fish hit my spinner. *Damn, that looked like a Brown,* I thought, *a small Brown, but a Brown.* Reality told me I didn't know for sure, but I chose to believe it was a trout.

I skipped the next two likely spots to get to one that looked special. Slowly, I worked my way along the inside of a hairpin bend. When I got to the center I dropped my spinner close to the beginning of the undercut bank. I could sense that fish were there, but if my instinct was right, the fish were too smart to get fooled by a little flashy metal. So much for my ability to think like a fish. It was almost noon. *I'm out of here.*

Day 2

I couldn't get The Little Elkhart out of my mind. In spite of my lack of success, I liked her. *She was like a clever woman shielding her brood, protecting her treasures. I just needed to uncover her secrets.* Was it wishful thinking to believe trout had to be there? Could be; the stream deserves a second look.

The first Saturday in September was cool with a little drizzle. *Perfect,* I like to fish on dreary days. I arrived before dawn and was suited up with waders on at first light. I made my way upstream to the spot where I'd sensed "fish had to be." Standing at the same spot where I'd failed two weeks before and using my fly rod, I carefully dropped a nymph fly at the beginning of the run. The results were the same: no runs, no hits, not even an error. *Time to move on.*

Undiscouraged, I resumed my quest. The more I saw of the stream, the better I liked her. Clear cold water racing beneath the surface cutting into banks, under the logs and brush, down the runs forming pools that swirled deep before moving on to create another hideaway. *If it only had a few fish.*

It must have been about nine-thirty, the drizzle had turned to a light rain, the woods had evolved into meadow with a corn field in the distance. I was moving along a slow stretch of stream that offered little promise. I casually flipped my spinner under the only tree at the edge water. Bam, fish on. *"Woo, hold on there little fella',"* I said out loud. This was a Brown, about ten inches I guessed, as he passed me heading downstream. He had plenty of running room because the stream was clear of obstacles compared to the stream flowing through the woods. I took him and a twin from the same unlikely spot. *Why would any self-respecting trout be in this marginal water, when there were a multitude of hiding places downstream?* I waded over to see what was so special about the water under the tree.

When I reached the exact spot where the fish hit, I could see a subtle difference in the bottom. The sand seemed to have a trench with more pebbles on the bottom. It looked about a foot deep, maybe five feet wide, and fifteen feet long, possibly more. At first I couldn't figure out why the bottom would be dug-out in that area. Then I saw a trickle of water coming from the bank just above where the trench began; where the fish were lurking. Curious to find the source of this trickle, I crawled over the bank and followed the water for about a city block. The origin was a little circular pool about three feet in diameter. Peering into the pool, I saw the sand was bubbling at the bottom and I realized it was a spring. *Oh my, how beautiful! I'll bet only a handful of people will get to see this beauty. Thanks, God.* I thought, privileged to be one of them.

The spring's flow not only dug the trench, but sent colder water into the stream. I guess the trout liked that. I was elated. *There were trout in Indiana.*

Little did I know at the time, that the meandering Little Elkhart, a gentle stream, with subtle nuances, would become my all-time favorite trout stream. *Not for the fish I caught, but for the fish I knew were there but couldn't catch.*

That first year, I returned to The Little Elkhart every Saturday I could get away. I found several places to get on the stream, all better than the park.

When I asked the Amish farmers' permission to cross their land and fish on their stream, the best part of the river in my opinion, they looked at me like I was a nut case. Apparently they were too busy farming to consider such nonproductive nonsense worthwhile. They ignored me most of the time, except, when they saw me heading for the stream, they would shake their heads and smile; seldom wave or say a word.

I like the Amish, they seemed to have a pure understanding of what's important, and they live according to their values. Independence personified, and they figured out how to keep Big Brother at bay.

I caught three more Browns that September, and I caught a couple Brookies in the smaller upstream water above the Emma fork. I never caught a Brook trout after that first year. I assume either the water got too warm as woods was replaced with farm land, or the planted fish, Browns, were better suited to the stream. Too bad, but Browns are my favorite species because they are usually too smart to fall for my offerings.

In October, I began to catch a few very nice fish, in the fourteen-inch range. The more I fished the stream the more solidly hooked I became.

A really pleasant surprise was discovering that, unlike in Wisconsin, the season closed at the end of December rather than on Halloween. After a sluggish summer, November proved exceptional. On Thanksgiving morning I took four good fish, one close to eighteen inches with a hefty girth. When I gutted him I thought triumphantly, *I'd like to see how big your sisters are.* I figured the bigger Browns, being fall spawners, had worked their way upstream to find cool clean water with a pebbly bottom.

And, I knew where, at least, a few of them gathered.

On my way to the car it dawned on me that I hadn't seen another fisherman, or even a boot print from that very first day at the park. *This is good.*

New Years came.

Spring couldn't come fast enough. But when it did . . .

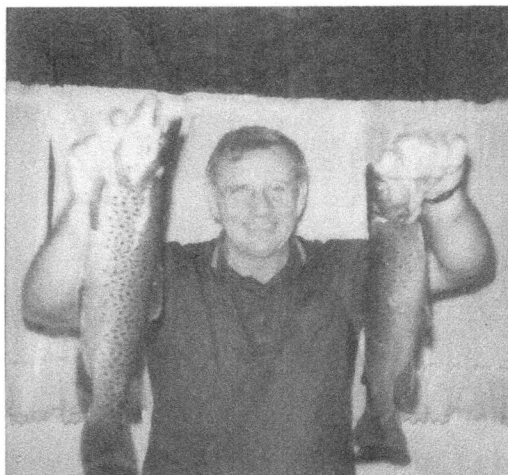

Indiana Year 2 - Opening Day

I drove by Middlebury Park just before dawn. The parking lot was half-filled with cars. Opening day experiences in Wisconsin should have prepared me, but after not seeing a single fisherman last year, I didn't expect the volume of fisherman would be so heavy. *My, oh my,* I said to myself, *This is not going to be pretty.* Cars and pickup trucks lined both sides of the road close to the Emma and Little Elkhart fork. *Not good, better move on.*

I waved to the family in the solid black Amish buggy as we past on the dirt road that led to their farm. Again, vehicles more old than new were parked every which way. *No need to go farther.* I pulled over at the end the line.

Suited up, I trudge down to the stream, walking with two other late comers. They reminded me of Laurel and Hardy. "Hey, Mister, how ya' doin'?" said the skinny one I mentally named Stan Laurel, "Ready to catch a mess of them fish."

"We'll see." I said smiling at the similarity.

"You will," the Hardy character said, as he raised his brows with an "Oliver" twinkle in his all-knowing eyes. They were both dressed in blue jeans, work shoes, and carried old-fashion rod and reels. Laurel swung a metal bucket in rhythm to his bouncy pace. A small Hill's Brothers coffee can, I assumed was filled with worms, was in the bucket. "Good luck," they said enthusiastically as we parted.

When I hit the stream, I realized I was the one out of place. No one wore waders; few wore hip boots. Bank fishermen were evenly spaced along a section of slow water that ran through the Amish farmer's pasture. I walked downstream staying several yards back from the bank, hoping that when I reached the woods I'd find less traffic.

Before I got to the woods a redheaded, pimple-faced teenager with a grin plastered all over it, was coming from where I was going. "Any luck?" I said.

The grinner held up a chain stringer with five Rainbow trout dangling at the end. All five looked identical; a little short of ten inches. *Kind of thin,* I thought, *even for Rainbows.*

"They're even bigger than the ones I got last year." The grinner said, very pleased with his trophies. "And they're bitin' like nobody's business."

"Wow, that's great, would you mind telling me your secret."

"Corn," he smiled the smile of a master.

"Corn? What are they, vegetarians? I fished this stretch of stream last summer and never caught a single Rainbow."

Pimple face, looked at me like I was too stupid for words. "You can't catch trout in the Little Elkhart in the summer, man."

"I can't?"

"You gotta get 'em now."

"I do?"

"Ya, ya do, the State Conservation people planted 'em about a month ago. The really good fishing is always opening day, morning's the best."

"That's it? Fish today and the season's over?"

"Well, a few guys fish for a couple more weeks, but I could never catch shit after opening day weekend. I don't think they get many after that either."

"Too bad," I said, "I guess I'll mosey on down into the woods," thinking, *thank God I won't be seeing this yo-yo on the stream again.*

"Good luck," he said as we parted.

Almost every fisherman I passed had a few of those cookie cutter Rainbows, and everybody seemed to be using bait. Could it be that mine was the only fly rod on the stream? When I got into the heart of the woods, I found every spot occupied. *What the hell am I doing here?* I turned around and started heading back to my car. When I got to almost the same spot, the pimply redhead, the yo-yo, was heading toward me again.

"Goin' back for more?" I couldn't help but smile.

"Yup, got those babies on ice. You gonna fish?"

"Na, no corn."

"I'll be glad to give you some," he said excitedly.

"Thank you, my friend, but I've decided to go to breakfast and let the stream clear out a little."

"Okay. I'll be in the woods, if you change your mind."

"Thanks." With that, I made my way to the car.

The welcoming smell of frying bacon raised my spirits when I opened the restaurant door. The only open seat was in the middle of, what I hoped was, a group table. It was.

"Come on over, buddy," a pudgy guy said pointing to the chair across from him. It turned out that I was sitting in the locals table, a congenial lot who sat together every Saturday. None of them was Amish, but they were part of the small business community scattered around the area. I introduced myself. They nodded and smiled as one riddled off their first names.

I listened with little interest to a group critique of Notre Dame's recent success in basketball. When there was a lull in the chatter, I said, "I was hoping to fish the river but a herd of fisherman beat me to it."

"You must be new here," Brian, the guy at the head of the table said.

"I am, but I fished there last Fall. Didn't see a soul."

"You won't in the Fall, but you can thank the State Conservation people for the mess they've made of opening day," Brian said. "It's a game."

"What do you mean?"

"I mean, sure as I'm sittin' here, every spring the state natural resources people plant a boo-coo number of 'put-and-take' Rainbows in the creek a few weeks before the season opens. Every yahoo with a rod will believe he's a trout fisherman because he can catch a few pellet fed, pampered fish that have no idea how to survive on their own. Hell, those fish, they'll eat anything."

"They do this every year?"

"Yup, that's the game. Money," Brian said. "The Rainbows don't reproduce or even adjust well enough to survive. Their only function is to generate license buyers and the money, in turn, goes to finance the state department of natural resources. It's not like we're in Colorado," he continued. "Cold mountain streams are where Rainbows actually survive. This is flatland, corn country, bass, brim, catfish country. But, as long as they keep raising put-and-take Rainbows, they have a job."

"I see your point." Finding a kindred spirit, I smiled and said "You seem to know a lot about the Little Elkhart. Do you fish it?"

"Did, til my knees gave out. Too much climbin' around for me now."

The breakfast was great. It was about ten-thirty when I drove back to the stream. Half the cars were gone, but I'd lost my enthusiasm. I went back home, wrote the day off as a re-learning experience, promising never to fish opening day again, no matter how long the winter.

Fishing - Freedom Lost

Government bureaucrats:
Manage, or mismanage, the streams.
Force us to pay for the privilege of fishing.

They control:
How many fish will be in the stream,
What sections we are allowed to fish,
How many fish we can keep – if any,
How big or small they have to be,
What days and, sometimes even, what hours we
can fish.
What lures we can use and how many barbs can
be on the lure.

We unknowingly elect dupes who unwittingly
create rules that rob us of our freedom and then
police us to make sure we march in step and
guarantee they get their due.

They Always Come Back

There is evidence trout, like salmon, will always return to where they were born when it comes their time to spawn. In my mind, I've taken that notion a step beyond science. With absolutely no evidence to back it up, I'm convinced that female trout, once they that find a spot they like, will lay their eggs in the exact spot every year from then on – getting bigger every year. This concept, or maybe just a wishful illusion, is fodder for my active imagination in the off-season.

Feeder streams, like the ones on the Little Elkhart, vary in size from little creeks to trickles of spring fed water. It's there that amorous Browns rub together in their mating dance. Just below where the feeders merge with the main stream, Browns gather to catch their breath before and after the spawning ritual. It's those staging areas that, I believed, harbored trophy trout.

****

After three years fishing the Little Elkhart, I realized I'd become infatuated with her subtle idiosyncrasies. She is a beautiful lady in motion, shifting sand in whirling current, evolving, ever changing, a delicate power, a treasure. Little did I know that my love affair with the Little Elkhart would last more than twenty years.

It was Christmas eve morning. A blanket of fresh snow covered crispy leaves that crunched under my clunky wader boots. I'd never fished trout with snow on the ground before because I lived in Wisconsin where the season closed at the end of October. It was a new feeling; the whitened ground, the brittle air, I liked it.

I figured the Browns were about done spawning for the year. They begin to show up in the staging areas toward the end of September and usually hang around until a week or so after Thanksgiving. After a couple of unsuccessful hours, I decided to check out Emma Creek. Emma is actually the north fork of the Little Elkhart. I'd been planning to explore it for quite some time, but it was just far enough upstream that, I never got around to it – today was the day.

The walk upstream was easier than I expected. The snowy bank was high enough that I could easily survey the entire bottom. The view revealed several spots that looked good enough to fish, but I resisted until I got to the fork where Emma Creek and Rowe Eden Ditch join to form the main body of Little Elkhart. The deep pool created by the current from the two streams merging was just too good to pass up.

Slipping down the bank, I realized how much easier it was to fish this section of the stream than the woods that had occupied most of my time. A weighted nymph was attached to the leader. *This will do it for a start*, I thought.

After a few back casts, my fly plopped noisily about ten feet above the hole. *Not good.* I stripped line quickly as the fly raced to the hole. Seeing the line come to a stop, I thought I was hung up on a snag. When I pulled the line tight, the snag darted down stream. *Fish on,* not that my technique deserved it. A good fish, not huge, ran down and across the hole with creative zigs and zags. I enjoyed the maneuver. When he finally tired, I slipped my net under him with a smile. *I'm not gonna be skunked today, Merry Christmas.*

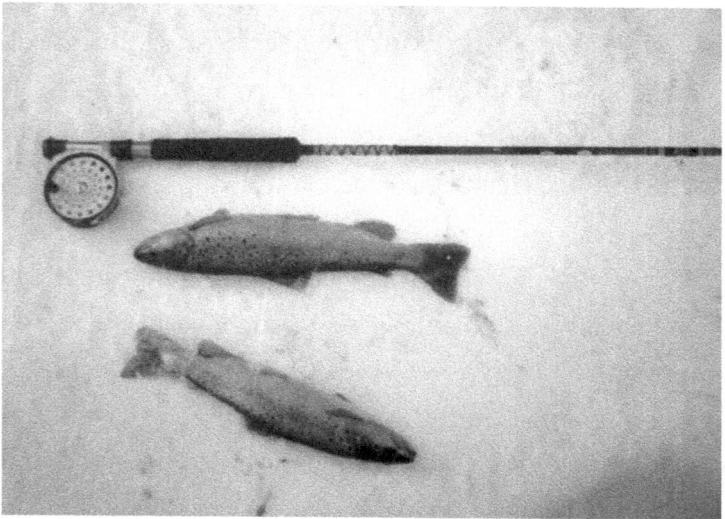

Ten minutes later twin Browns nestled in the creel.

Better move on, or I'll never see what Emma has to offer.

Emma Creek was smaller than I thought it would be. Several straight shallow runs flowed along Amish farm fields. I wasn't impressed. When I got to a scrubby wooded section the stream began to snake its way around obstacles. *This is more like it,* I thought. Each turn dug deep into the bank creating dark pockets that, I imagined, must harbored granddaddy trout.

Slowly and quietly, I positioned myself behind and across from the first turn. My fly landed softly. *Perfect*, I thought. The second cast was just as good. After giving the hole ample effort, I moved upstream to the next bend. Same effort, same result. As my confidence dwindled, I started to move from one bend to the next without taking the time to give my best effort.

I was at the last bend in the woods when a fish jolted my rod. *Holy mackerel, what's this?* The stream was small and narrow – the fish was big and smart. He took me upstream; I held him tight. Then he darted back into the deepest darkest part of the undercut bank where tree roots stuck out and brush hung over the edges. The big fish had me hung up on something, but I could still feel him pumping and pulling, trying to get loose.

After we both tried and failed to free the line, I decided to attempt to get my net under him. I moved to the shallow-side bank and took off my hunting jacket, pulled my waders up to the max, and moved as close to the pocket as I could get. I could see the fish. He could see me. I poked my net into the water extending my arm as deep as I dared without water going over my boots. *Cold, damn cold.*

I couldn't get the net deep enough to succeed, but, I guess it was deep enough to inspire the Brown to find the power to snap the end of my leader.

You win for now, but I'll be back next year.

They always come back – I will be waiting.

Superior Angler

Each of us rubber clad "Isaac Walton" clones establish a routine we honed into, what we call, our special technique. This unique skill was acquired or developed over years of "trial and error" and dumb luck – when we accidentally stumbled onto something that actually enticed the fish to take a chance.

Many of us believe our routine is superior to that of other anglers. We are puzzled when our fishin' buddies get back to the car with heavy creels and ours is barely damp. Whenever that happens, we, all too often, mentally write it off as dumb luck, never admitting to having inferior methods. And – God forbid, we are much too macho to ask how they caught their treasure.

Even if a friendly novice were shameless enough to ask, we know damn well he wouldn't get an honest answer. The master would rather admit to a venereal disease than share the actual details.

The only exception to this peculiar custom may be a father fishing with a young son. But, once the offspring out fishes the father, school's over.

So much for that bit of philosophical babble.

Perch

"Coo, coo, coo," A mourning dove, my summertime alarm clock, was trying to coax me out from under my cozy covers. I didn't jump right out of bed because I loved to lay there and listen to that mysterious lonely call. It's still my favorite sound.

It was summer and I was free to run wild once I got past my oatmeal and grapefruit. I hated the tart taste but my mom loaded it with sugar. I always made a sourpuss face when I gulped it down just to make sure an ample amount of sugar would be piled on next time.

The year was 1948 and I was an eleven-year-old. No one bothered to ask what I did all day as long as I got home in time for supper. The evening meal was called supper, lunch, as I remember it, was a peanut butter sandwich and an apple.

There were eight of us: Mom and Dad, my two sisters, Grandma, Grandpa Dick, Aunt Mary, dad's sister, and me, all crammed into Grandpa's six-room house with a spooky crawl space under the floor. It would be considered small according to today's standards. Back then, size didn't seem all that important.

Bam, the screen door slammed as I jumped over the three porch steps and hit the grass in full stride. In those days I started my days on the run. My escape was clean before dishes or a list of chores materialized. Crisp cool air felt so good I took extra deep breaths as I sprinted to the Millar house.

Roger Millar and I, the youngest members of the neighborhood gang, were considered insignificant by Roger's older brother Gene and his macho cohorts. Gene, two years older and a foot taller, was the undisputed gang leader.

The enchanted morning was spoiled when I learned that Gene and company were already off to whatever mischief they could conger up. Roger and I had been left behind.

After a sufficient period of moping, Roger's mother, aware of our disappointment, said, "Hey you sourpusses, how'd you like to take a boat out."

"That would be great, Mom," Roger said, "You think it would be okay with Dad?"

Roger's dad, I called him old man Millar, had built eight flat bottom wooden row boats that he rented out to local fisherman. We kids were almost never allowed to use a boat. This was indeed a special day.

"You gonna get the oars?" she said, ignoring the question. "Skedaddle, before I change my mind."

Behind Millar's garage there was a pile of last fall's leaves mixed with an assortment of select garbage put there to attract worms. Roger turned the mulchy concoction with a pitchfork and I, sitting on my heels, snatched worm after worm until the old coffee can was over half full.

We picked cane poles from a tangled clump stored in a back corner of the garage, checked to make sure they had a hook, sinker, and cork bobber, grabbed a big bucket and ran down to the dock. Roger pointed to the only boat with a dry bottom. "That one."

Standing on the long narrow plank that separated ours from the other boats, I handed Roger our gear one item at a time. Then, with a bit of anxiety, I carefully stepped into the boat keeping one hand holding tight on the side.

Roger, now the captain, said, "Sit in the back seat, I'll shove us off." He put the end of an oar on the shore and gave a mighty push. When boat cleared the dock, current grabbed it, gently taking us downstream. *Roger and I had been fishing lots a times from the bank, or from railroad bridge trestles, but never in a boat. And we seldom caught more than a fish or two.*

Roger, much to my surprise, knew how to row. I guess his mom must have known that all along. With a grin on his face, he pulled each oar in opposite directions, and we turned completely around. Heading upstream he said, "I know a spot, even Gene doesn't know about."

Skeptical, I said, "How'd you find it?" After all, only Gene knew everything; Roger and I were just dumb tag-a-longs.

"Two old timers rented one of our boats last summer on a Sunday morning when everybody was at church except me. I can't remember how I got out of going, but anyway, I watched 'em from the railroad bridge. And, they caught a mess of perch."

I was still suspicious. At that age we all made stuff up, at least I did, so I was pretty sure Roger did, too. Rodger was heading right for the bridge which didn't make sense to me because we could fish from the bridge without a boat, but he was the captain, I was happy to be along for the ride. When we went under the bridge, I couldn't keep my mouth shut any longer. "Roger, where you goin'? Nobody fishes above the bridge."

"The old timers did, and I know right where they anchored."

The little bay he took us to was formed when land had been extended before the actual railroad bridge began. I, along with the rest of the gang, had walked down the tracks above the little bay hundreds of times. It wasn't very big and didn't go out very far from shore.

We were twenty yards, well upstream from the bay, when Roger turned around in his seat, moved forward on his knees, picked up a makeshift anchor, a big rock tied to the end of an eight foot rope, and dropped it over the side. We quickly stopped drifting with the current. Roger pointed to the anchor under my seat, "Drop that one too," he said.

"Why do we need two?" I said after seeing how big my rock anchor was.

"It'll keep us from swaying."

We were at a spot downstream from where Lake Winnabago crashes over a spillway dam and becomes the Fox River. It rushes over the shallow flat and under Neenah, Wisconsin's main street bridge at a pretty good clip; without a second anchor the boat would swing back and forth.

My rock was so heavy I just managed to get it over the side. As I let out rope the anchor seemed to get lighter and lighter. *I must be getting stronger*, I thought. When it hit bottom, the rope went taut pulling hard on the eyelet fastened to the back corner of the boat.

"Toss me a worm," Roger said moving to the front seat.

Mimicking Roger, I strung the worm on the hook, took off our cork, and dropped the line over the side until the sinker hit bottom. Next I forced the line back into the slit in the cork, positioning it so the hook would be about six inches off the bottom. I no sooner had raised the line when a fish tried to pull it from my hand. "Roger, look at this," I shouted.

"Pull him in, dumbo."

Hand over hand, I pulled the seven-inch Perch to the surface and hoisted him into the boat. By the time I landed mine, Roger had caught one even bigger. "Put some water in the bucket," he said.

Leaning over the edge of the boat, which was kind of scary, I lifted the bucket over the side and water began to gush in. It got heavy fast, too fast to handle. *Oh, oh, I'm in trouble.* Panicky, I pulled on the handle with all my might and, splashing plenty of water out, I just managed it back over the side and into the boat. Roger never knew how close I came to falling out of the boat trying to save that damn bucket. When I put the fish in the water, one jumped out. I scrambled to pick the flopper up and stuck him back; he jumped out again. I stuck him again. He was out in seconds. *Okay then,* I thought, *Suck air, see if I care.*

By the time I gave up on gettin' the fish in the pail, Roger caught another one.

Re-wormed, my enthusiasm was rewarded before the sinker hit the bottom. Wham, *This is no Perch,* I thought holding tight as the tip of my bamboo pole dipped into the water. I pulled hard. He pulled harder. I pulled harder yet. The pole bent to the rhythm of the fish's maneuvers. It bowed with every dart and relaxed when the fish charged toward me. Ooh, how I loved the feel of that fish pumping the wispy old bamboo pole. Today, when I have a Trout testing my highfalutin', overpriced, fly rod it feels almost as good as that precious old bamboo – but not quite.

The fish, by the way, was a Rock Bass, some people call them red-eye, maybe 10" at best. But, he fought like a Tasmanian devil, with a determination even big Perch lack.

As I remember it, there was seldom a pause between

bites and very few fish got away. We pulled in one after another for what seemed to be hours. At the end of the morning, our bucket was filled with more fish than water. The worms were gone. It was time to go home. God had smiled down on a couple of happy river-rats; for me, it was a precious moment in a time.

When I ran home to boaster my half of the fish, my mother and Grandpa Dick made a huge fuss over my accomplishment. After Grandpa Dick showed me how, I scaled and gutted every last one of them, no matter how small.

At dinner that night the chatter was about how I provided the food. After usually being ignored, I was elated to be appreciated as a provider.

When I look back on that experience today, it dilutes the "catch and release" philosophy being portrayed as the way of the modern sportsman.

Although today I occasionally fish "Catch and Release" streams, the experience will never be as rewarding as when I'm lucky enough to catch a few using the philosophy nature provides. Catch, Clean, and Eat.

The most successful Trout fishermen
are the most creative.
They persistently vary old techniques,
and invent new ones in their quest.

Ruby Sue Tootser

Instinct

We just had to do it

When a Wisconsin Winter relents to Spring, the March sun begins to penetrate the two-foot icecap on Lake Winnabago. As winds shift, the ice breaks up into huge pieces that crash over the spillway and through the gates at the Neenah Dam. The swirling current of the Fox River carries the mammoth slabs of ice downstream bouncing and banging like an arcade pinball machine. The river races North to Green Bay, where the once powerful ice islands float into Lake Michigan, dwindle, and become a teeny part of the vast body of water.

A few weeks later Perch gather in schools and begin their journey upstream to spawn. They find man-built dams hinder their efforts to find the marshes of the headwaters, the natural place to deposit their spawn. Time after time the schools of Perch charge upstream with all the power mating species possess. And time after time, unlike the powerful Trout and Salmon, the amorous Perch are turned back at the damn dam.

Unlike today's kids, I, along with the other neighborhood hooligans roamed the banks and bridges of the Fox, without parents showing an inkling of concern. In the mid-1940s, without TV, cell phones, or namby-pamby organized programs, we were FREE to invent own world and establish our own priorities.

One find day my friend Roger and I, and Gene, Roger's older brother, were out on the railroad bridge that serviced a paper mill across the river. The old wooden bridge crossed the Fox about a half-mile downstream from the dam – our neighborhood. We considered it our bridge since we spent endless hours fishing from, and climbing over, under and around every inch of it. It was a boy's paradise.

The bridge was built on huge cedar pylons that looked like sawed off telephone posts placed in lines that formed sections about thirty feet apart. The sections were capped with huge rectangular timber that extended well past the width needed for the tracks. Centered directly under where the tracks would go, several, I can't remember how many, probably six, thirty foot massive rectangular timbers were equally spaced between the sections. Railroad ties topped it off. They seemed to be spaced just far enough apart that they were hard to walk on.

"Holy shit," Roger said, leaning over a flimsy rail on a walk on one side of the bridge.

"What?" I said, looking down into the swift clear water below.

"There," Roger pointed, "the school of fish."

"Wow, there's thousands of them. Let's get our poles," I said.

It was a natural instinct most boys seemed to have. If fish were there, we needed to catch them. And – it wasn't up to government bureaucrats to tell us when we could fish, how many we could take, or by what means we used to get the fish.

"You can't catch those sons-a-bitches," The all-knowing Gene, said with his usual smirk, "They won't bite 'til they're done spawnin'."

"You sure?" I asked, before I realized you never question the all-knowing.

"Don't you think I'd be fishing if you could catch the sons-a-bitches." He gave me *his stupid little jerk* glare.

"Maybe we can net 'em," Roger said trying to bail me out.

"And just where in the hell are we gonna get a net, Dick-head," Gene said. Roger and Gene always seemed to be on opposite sides, but they would defend each other to the death, if they thought the other was being threatened. Having no brothers, I couldn't understand their relationship.

We stood there watching schools of Perch charge upstream in bursts going under the bridge through one section, then drifting back in the section closest to shore.

I don't remember who had the idea, probably Gene. He was a jerk but he was a smart jerk. First, we built a dam across the section where the fish drifted back. It was less than two-feet deep even on the far side and, using the bigger rocks scattered along the tracks on shore, it didn't take long. We left an opening in the dam, about thirty-inches wide hoping fish would drift back through it. Gene found some old fencing used for a rabbit hutch and bent it into a long circular shape. He bent the wire inward at one end to form a bottom and left the other end open. He attached a rope to the front edge of his newly created basket. Beaming, he said, "That ought to get those sons-a-bitches."

While Gene built the trap, Roger and I managed to pinch two long planks from a pile neatly stacked behind old man Shabo's garage. Shabo was a cranky old neighbor who was always yelling at us for one thing or another. In retrospect, he probably was the only neighbor that had an inkling what our band of thieves was up to.

The planks were long enough to fit between the timbers that capped the pilings forming a ledge below the walkway.

On hands and knees, Gene crawled out on the planks holding the rope with the basket swinging freely below.

"Drop it, Gene," I said filled with anticipation.

"Keep your pants on butt head," he responded as he lowered the basket into the current behind the opening in the dam. He tightened the rope a little, pulling the basket snuggly against the opening. "That son-of–a-bitch is gonna get those sons-a-bitches," Gene said with a convincing smile.

Roger and I nodded agreement. It was a perfect fit. Now it was up to the fish.

We no more than had everything set when a huge school drifted into the front of the section between the pilings. "Come on you sons-a-bitches," Gene was as intent as a dog on point. The school drifted to the front of the basket going from side to side, moving forward a few yards, and drifting back again. Gene whispered, "Come on you sons-a- . . . ." The school surged forward out of the section, out of sight, out of danger.

"Shit, shit, shit," Roger said. "They're too smart to go into the basket."

A short minute went by that felt like an hour. The school was back in the section. Again they surged forward and drifted back each time coming closer to the basket. Then slowly the Perch began to drift into basket. Six, ten, twenty. "Holy crap," Roger said in awe. The trap had worked, it was filled with fish. "Pull the son-of-a-bitch," I screamed at Gene.

He pulled with all his might and the front of the basket trap popped up and out of the water. "Shit," Gene shouted, "It's too damn heavy to get out of the water. Climb your asses down there and help me get the son-of-a-bitch to the shore."

Roger scrambled back along the planks to the pilings. We managed to crawl over the edge and down along a diagonal support to the edge of the section on top of the makeshift dam. It practically gave way as we got to the basket. Damn that water was cold. Together we grabbed the rope and made our way back to the pilings. Gene followed us down once we controlled the basket. He grabbed the end of the rope, and together we dragged the basket ashore.

Wide eyed, we admired our catch. "I'll be a son- - -of- - -a- - -bitch," Gene said in a slow staccato whisper.

"Roger, go get a bucket and hurry. You," he said pointing in my face, "start rebuilding the dam. And, we're gonna need more than one rope on this son-of-a-bitch."

Roger came running with a five-gallon bucket in hand.

At the water's edge he scooped a little water in. "About a third full," Gene commanded.

Who made you the boss, asshole, Roger thought with an unfriendly glare.

We quickly scooped the Perch out of the basket and into the pail. "We're gonna need a bigger pail," I said stating the obvious. Water was running over the side and fish were flopping out of the pail as we added perch.

Roger went for another bucket, Gene and I repaired the dam and we added more ropes to the basket. We were back in business. We got a few more baskets of fish but the numbers were small compared to that first catch. By the end of the day we filled two five-gallon buckets with fish without adding water. We offered fish to all the neighbors including Mr. Shabo. They all thanked us and no one asked where the fish came from or why they were still filled with spawn. They were just happy to be included. Old man Shabo didn't bitch about us for a few days, not that we cared but our parents undoubtedly did. We went back the next day, but the run was over.

I doubt that Gene knew what "sons-of-bitches" actually meant and I know his mom, a wonderful Christian woman, would have been horrified if she heard him. But, after all being chief merited tough talk. And, like it or not, he was our leader.

Gene's on the left with the hat. I'm on the far right and Roger is in the back looking over my shoulder and the shoulder of Tommy McGee, not mentioned in the story. I don't remember who the little kid was.

We built the raft using who knows whose lumber, but there had to be some major wood under that deck to float four of us, probably more at times.

What freedom boys had in those days, what creativity we were allowed to implement. Kids today live a structured existence, protected at the cost of creative freedom. Are we thwarting the development of the problem solving gene in our future entrepreneurs? *Could be.*

My First Trout

I was lucky at a young age to have the opportunity to travel out west with my folks. My dad ran his own advertising agency that would frequently have perks; in this case he did some artwork for new condos up on Brian Head Mountain in Utah. I had no idea what to expect when we got there and had only seen the brochures that Dad worked on. The images showed a large condominium nestled in the woods with snow peaked mountains in the background. I couldn't wait to get there...

It was sometime in the summer of 1979 when the news of going on a trip to Utah was brought up. I was 10 years old and, several days before the trip, Dad was brainstorming ideas on maps. This was a ritual for him before any trip. Ah, the old map ritual... He would spread out maps on his art board in the family room, like a boat captain plotting a great sea voyage. Whistling to himself and drawing his fingers along roads and rivers running all directions. "We could take this route once we get out of

Nevada and probably get to this lake over here . . . or we could go north to blah blah blah…" It didn't really matter to me, I just wanted to get there! But to him, it was endless routes and possibilities.

If you were to give my dad a map of the state you lived in or any old map, prepare yourself for Captain Bob, the navigator, because he will discover new and alternate routes that you probably didn't even know existed! Anyway, you get the idea. Dad is a map nut. Besides all the map prepping, we had several hyped discussions regarding fishing for trout in various streams or mountain lakes. By the time we were done talking about fishing, I was pretty jacked up to go.

We flew out of Chicago O'Hare airport late morning and arrived in Las Vegas Nevada early afternoon. We grabbed our luggage and hustled to the car rental shuttle service. We ended up with a full- size sedan in what I now call rental red in color. For whatever reason, I do not know, burgundy cars with burgundy interior make me want to vomit! Maybe it's just a coincidence, but it seemed like every time we got a rental car, it would be in this color combination, nasty red, and the interior always smelled funky or smoky. Luckily for me, my Mom was prepared from previous trips in such cars and brought the Dramamine.

"Thanks Mom!" Once we got situated with the car, it was back to map time… or captain Bob! "Ok, Baylor," Dad referred to my mom as, Baylor, her maiden name.

"We could take this road north to Panguitch Lake and get a bite to eat there, or head east and go blah, blah, blah...

"Let's just get to the condo first," I suggested.

"Okay then," dad replied. We headed northeast on Interstate 15 and grabbed a bite to eat in Cedar City. Not having much to eat on the plane, we swiftly scarfed our meals down and got back on the road.

The road we were now on was getting more twists, turns, and steeper in elevation. As we continued to climb, I noticed there were very few guard rails, if any at all, to keep us from flying off the edge. "Holy shit!" I thought to myself. The view, however, was breath taking. We could see Cedar Breaks in the distance which was a colorful canyon on the edge of Brian Head Mountain. Eventually we got to a lookout spot that gave you a grand view of the canyon. I'm not a huge fan of heights, but I did get out of the car to look at Cedar Breaks, or should I say, crawled out to the railing where they had the viewing area.

"Holy crap! This is high up." Hands sweating and heart pounding, I continued to inch forward to get a good look. Dad gave a shout out over the canyon echoing, "Hello-hello-hello-hello."

Of course I responded back, "Hey-hey-hey-hey." The orange and red cathedral canyon was vast and deep, a portrait of some of God's artwork.

Not far from this colorful playground was Brian Head Mountain, which can be seen from Cedar Breaks, just off to the right. The condo was just a hop, skip and a jump away. We continued up the mountain road until we came upon a resort area nestled in the mountain woods. It was a new ski resort that was just being built. The roads were all dirt and reminded me of an old Western setting at first glimpse. We pulled up to the condo and got out of the car to stretch. The air was thin and crisp, with a subtle hint of pine scent.

"This is awesome!" I said. The building was cedar-toned with large stone pillars out front giving it a northern cabin feel that was warm and inviting.

We grabbed our luggage and settled in our cozy room for the evening and went over potential fishing spots. Thumbing through the maps, Dad said, "I think we should take a look at Panguitch Lake, also it looks to me like there's a creek that runs into it that might be worth looking at."

I nodded my head in agreement.

"Okay then," Dad said, "we'll go to Cedar City in the morning for breakfast and get fishing licenses while were at it."

So we got up around 9-ish the next morning and headed towards town to grab breakfast and all our fishing needs. Afterward, we got back on 15 to Route 143 to Panguitch Lake. The scenery was beautiful as the road cut through red rock canyons and forest. The lake was huge, settled in a little mountain valley surrounded with tall pines, rocks and scrub brush that gave it a wild remote look. We found a restaurant bar and grill close by, and my dad talked to some of the locals who were fishing earlier in the day.

According to their story, nobody was catching anything. Typical response from locals to an outsider, they may or may not be catching fish. Dad gave kind-of, a "humph" response to it all.

"Well," Dad said, "let's just grab a bite to eat and we'll take a look at the map again to see how far the creek runs out of the lake?" We ordered burgers and looked over the trusty map... all kidding aside, my Dad was a wiz with maps and usually hit his mark on deciding best routes and fishing spots.

After lunch we followed Panguitch Creek north of the lake. It weaved gently through the vast mountains and wilderness. We finally parked alongside of the road.

"This is it, looks like a great spot to me." I was ready to fish!

We got our gear out, which was collapsible fishing rods, an assortment of number "0" Mepps spinners, long pants, two pairs of old sneakers to wade in the water, and straw cowboy hats to keep the sun off our necks.

As we started to walk towards the stream, Dad was explaining to me what spots to look for. "Look for deep pockets in the areas where the creek bends, trout like to hole-up in those spots. They also like cover where there's vegetation or branches overhanging the edges. Just make sure you don't walk into these spots. Move slowly, and try to be quiet so you don't spook 'em."

We split up. Dad went downstream, and I went a little

ways upstream in search of a good spot. The stream was bubbling and swiftly moving over the rocks, inviting me to get closer to investigate what might be around the corner.

This is it, I thought. A horseshoe-bend in the stream with a wide gravel edge for me to stand on. At the top of the bend, it looked like a deep pool about eight to ten feet in length. There was some vegetation hanging over the edges as well, offering plenty of cover. I carefully crept up to the gravel embankment and tied on a red and white #0 French spinner. My first cast didn't quite reach the pocket. "*Crap!*" I cast three or four more tries and same thing; kept landing short in shallow water. "*Alright, I gotta get in the water.*" So I moved downstream of the pocket a little, remembering Dad said the fish would be facing upstream.

I took a few steps into the water. *Whoa! That's frickin' cold! Alright, I can do this.* My first cast was the same as before, just a little short. *Gotta move up a bit.* The water wasn't getting any warmer and my legs were feeling a little numb from the cold, but I had a good feeling about this spot.

Next cast, bingo! Right where I wanted it. The little spinner landed right in the middle of the pocket. As I frantically reeled it in with anticipation, I wound up empty. "Maybe that was to fast?" I thought. Next cast landed up a little higher in the pocket and close to the edge. *Come on, come on, come on.* Wham! Fish on! I let out a big "Wahooo" that everyone could hear. The majestic Brown Trout was doing flips out of the water, and my heart was racing a mile a minute. The drag on my reel was whining while the fish ran for deeper water. *Come on buddy, come on.* I decided to back up quickly to get him in shallow water and fell right on my ass with all the excitement. I don't think I felt a thing.

Finally, I managed to horse my first trout onto the bank and let out another *Wahooo!*

And just like that, I was hooked!

*"My soul runs deep within the waters wherever
there are trout and these waters hold a treasure
full of memories that will last forever"*

Darin

Panguich Creek.

*"I love the environs where trout are found,
which are invariably beautiful,
and hate the environs where crowds
of people are found,
which are invariably ugly."*

Robert Traver

Little Big Waders

Iwas eleven going on eighteen when I went fishing with my Dad behind an old grocery store in Middlebury Indiana. We were fishing the Little Elkhart River, and I thought I knew everything after catching my first trout in Utah.

"Little did I know."

It was late September 1980, and I was ready to take on my next adventure into trout fishing. We got up around 6:30 A.M. and gathered up our gear to start our quest. Dad suggested getting breakfast in Middlebury before fishing and I agreed. So we headed off and came to a small-mom-and pop restaurant. Inside the dining area was the familiar smell of bacon and fresh brewed coffee. We both ordered bacon and eggs with rye toast; a coffee for him and I got hot chocolate.

Dad talked to me about the area we were going to fish and how he came to discover it years ago. He reminded me of how it will be much different than out west but the tactics would remain the same. "The biggest difference," he said, "is that the stream runs through a dense woods with a lot of heavy brush. It's damn easy to get turned around."

"I shouldn't have any problems," I remarked.

"No, I think you'll do fine; just stay close to the stream, and you can always follow it back to where you started."

"Ok…" After breakfast we headed towards our spot and approached a small family-owned grocery store. Behind it there was a large farm field with a two-track path cutting around it. Dad pulled around the building and headed right for the path. With a grimace on my face, I looked at my dad with approval of doing a little off-roading.

We weren't in your typical pickup truck, but a conversion van instead. No matter, it was pretty cool to me. Once we got to our parking spot I noticed the overgrowth of brush was eight feet tall, except for the matted down area we parked in. It was so thick that we could barely open the van doors to get out.

"Holy crap, this is thick!" I said. "How are we going to find our way through all this?"

Dad chuckled and said, "Well, once we plow through that tall crap over there for about twenty-five yards or so, we'll get to the stream; after that it's not too bad."

We started to get our gear out of the van. I was armed with a Daiwa ultra light spinning rod and reel with number zero and number one Mepps spinners in red and white, gold, and silver. I also brought my 7 ½ ft. fly rod with split shots and crawlers to drift into pockets.

The one thing that was not normal was the use of chest waders. Dad let me use a pair of his that fit in the feet but not so much in the waist. I had to use a belt to cinch together the upper part of the waders, so I could move about easier. "I feel like the Michelin Man!" I said laughing.

"Well, are ya ready?"

"Yup." I followed Dad through the dense brush that just happened to be riddled with a nasty weed that we call nettles. It felt like fiberglass insulation wherever it touched and, if you rubbed your skin one way, it felt like tiny needles burning into your skin. This stuff sucked!

Once we got to the stream, I noticed Dad washing and rubbing his arms and hands in the cold water. "This helps get the nettles out," he said.

I followed his lead. "Hope I don't run into more of that crap!"

"Me either, we'll have to pay attention to those coming back."

Dad gave me the rundown on the stream as far as using the water to find my way back if I get turned around. "Be careful getting in and out of the water," he cautioned, "avoid unnecessary slips, and at all cost avoid walking in the pockets. There are some very deep holes in this part of the stream, some that are over your head."

"Okay. I got it." I just wanted to get going.

"I'll head downstream a ways just to the other end of the woods," he said, "I think you'll have better luck upstream; we'll meet back at the van around ten o'clock."

We parted ways and my adventure began. The first thing I thought was to get out of the water to make sure I don't disturb the fish. As I looked for a spot to get out I noticed the embankments were steep. *This should be interesting*, I thought. How the heck am I going to get out with these frickin waders on? I grabbed on to a small sapling on the edge and pulled and crawled my way to the top; poles were clacking together and making all kinds of racket that I didn't want. Finally at the top I started to venture around the stream a ways.

I figured I would go upstream for awhile and work my way back to fish. Everything in these woods was overgrown and the oak trees were massive. Some of the trees I found had large thorns growing on them that looked like something from the Dark Ages. The farther I walked, the eerier it got. There were times that I had to backtrack because I lost a visual on the stream and got turned around. *Not a good feeling*. I felt really small in comparison to my surroundings and a little afraid of getting lost.

I decided to get in the stream and start hoofing it back a little ways where I was more comfortable. On my way back I found a couple nice pockets to fish but had no luck. *Probably spooked the fish*, I thought.

Alright then, I said to myself, *I'll sneak downstream a bit on the edge until I see another pocket.* About seventy-five yards down, I found a beauty. *This looks perfect!* Quietly approaching just upstream of the pocket, I knelt down and tied on a number zero red and white spinner. This was the same spinner I caught my first trout on; *this ought to work!*

First cast, I got hung up on some brush, "dang it." With a swift jerk of my ultra light, she was free. Second cast, wham! Fish on! This fish felt like a good one. My pole was bending and jerking all over the place. With all the excitement, I decided to get in the water to make sure I didn't lose the fish. Splash! In I went, the water was over my head and my waders were filling up. I thought I was a goner for sure. Frantically treading water, I put the fishing pole in my teeth and rode the pocket out until I could touch bottom again. Surprisingly the fish was still on my line! I got my footing back and gradually reeled him in to the edge.

"Holy smokes!" It was about a seventeen-inch Brown. Shaking like a leaf in a storm, I plopped the fish in my creel and immediately went looking for my dad. Both scared shitless and excited at the same time, I wanted to get to safety and show off my fish. I got out of the stream and started walking the edge downstream. Exhausted after walking, what felt like 10 miles, I saw him in the distance fishing.

I stopped and watched him for a bit, just to see how he does it. He was as quiet as a church mouse and moved through the woods like a deer, cautious, graceful, and with a purpose. I moved in a little closer and was spotted. "How did ya do?"

"Pretty good!" I proudly exclaimed. I told him how I caught my fish while treading downstream with my pole in my teeth. Dad was impressed and showed me his catch for the day. Three nice Browns lined his creel, all smaller than mine.

"Wow, nice catch!"

We decided to walk back on the outer edge of the woods alongside of the farmer's field. Talking about our adventure as we walked back, I never told my dad how scared I really was by myself that day. Only the fear of falling in the water was brought up.

The truth of the matter was, I was a little boy in a big boy's world. I thought I knew everything. I learned a lot that day.

Sometimes life requires you to put your big boy pants on and figure things out on your own, or in my case, big boy waders…

Chicken Coop

One of the more memorable places I recall fishing is a spot I called the chicken coop. This was a quiet remote place Dad had found on the Little Elkhart River close to our home in the state of Indiana. An Amish farmer granted him permission to walk on his land to get to the trout stream; the rub was, to get to the farm and stream, you had to walk behind a pole building next to the farm. It was being used as an industrial chicken coop with a ventilation system whose large fans kicked out an ammonia-based chicken shit smell that was unbearable. And, if that wasn't enough, a conveyor system dumped the waste at the back of the building. There must have been a thousand chickens in that building.

My first experience with this was a whole lot of cursing as we passed the vents. Dad smiled and threw in a few choice words of his own "Damn, that's a nasty smell. You just can't get used to it!"

He was right; that had to be the worst stench to come out of animals' behinds, or garbage dump, that I have ever been around.

I remember a time we invited Trevor, a good friend of mine, to go trout fishing with us. We picked him up around 7 A.M. On our way, we did our traditional stop at the local Dunkin' Doughnuts and picked up a half-dozen with coffee and hot chocolate. "Where's this place at?" Trevor asked.

"You'll see," I replied, knowing already his response should be fun to observe on our walk behind the coop. We got to our spot around 7:30, and Trevor was eager with anticipation. This was all a new experience for him to go trout fishing. Dad and I set him up with the appropriate gear; small ultra light rod and reel, French spinners, crawlers with small hooks and sinkers. Starting him off with a fly rod would have been a bit much. We also provided chest waders and, of course, Muskol, our number one choice for bug repellent.

We parked the van in a dirt drive next to the outbuilding that was the coop, gathered our gear, and slipped into our waders. "You ready?"

"Yup!" said Trevor.

Dad and I started to lead the way down the path behind the coop. I glanced back and saw Trevor bumbling around with his gear. "Come on, man!" I said.

"I'm coming, I'm coming!"

Not a minute later I glanced back again and noticed him slumped over by the huge pile of chicken shit at the back of the coop. He was puking his guts out and swearing up a storm.

Laughing my ass off, I ask, "Are you okay?"

"No, what the hell!" he replied.

I looked over at my dad and noticed his shoulders bouncing up and down with an inner chuckle. *This was not going so well,* I thought. It took a few minutes for Trevor to get over his slobbering puke fits and intermittent cursing, but eventually he made it through the gauntlet of chicken shit!

When we got to the stream, Dad broke off and headed downstream. I sent Trevor upstream a ways near a bridge. Before he started, I gave him a quick run down of how to cast his French spinner or bait upstream above the pockets where the trout may be. He wasn't too keen on this type of fishing, so I threw in a few other tips and tricks like moving slowly and quietly into the areas you're fishing and looking out for deep pockets with brush or vegetation for cover. Before I left him I added, "Make sure you don't step into the pockets you're fishing; you'll spook the fish."

"I got it." Trevor said with an *"enough already"* tone.

I wished him luck and started to work my way downstream. No more than two minutes went by and I heard him bumbling in the water and a splash! "You alright over there."

"Yup, I just slipped and got water in my waders."

Oh boy, I thought to myself, *this joker is going to dick up the whole morning.* I yelled over to him and told him, "Dump the water out on shore – come get me if you get into any more trouble, I'll be about 200 yards downstream, close to the pasture."

Trevor replied with an already discouraged, "Okay."

So – I finally got to my favorite spot and immediately

caught two Browns on a number one red and white fury Mepps. About five minutes later, bam! Another fish on. Nice Brown, *so far so good.* I fished another two hours in that area when Dad came slowly working his way toward me. "How many did ya get?"

"I caught four," I said beaming, "How about you?"

"Had one take a swipe at my fly, but that is about all she wrote."

"You might want to go to a spinner," I suggested.

"Na, you have enough fish for both of us. Besides, that sun is gettin' too high in the sky. Where's your buddy?"

"Good question, I figured he would be back by now."

We decided to go on a search for our new angler and low and behold we found him way off the beaten path, roaming around in another pasture heading in the opposite direction. I yelled out, "Trevor, over here!"

He looked up, waved, and started walking toward us. *Not much pep in that step,* I thought. By the time he finally made it back to us he was looking a little discombobulated and angry as hell. "I take it you didn't catch any fish?"

Trevor looked at me in disgust, "No I didn't catch any stinking fish."

"Come on, we got to get goin', it's time for lunch."

"I ain't goin' past that chicken coop, even if I have to stay out here the rest of my life."

"The bridge is about a quarter of a mile upstream," Dad said, "We'll pick you up there. Darin, maybe you can go with him."

"Okay. I can do that."

Trevor didn't say a word all the way to the bridge. Needless to say, I don't think we'll be taking my friend Trevor back here any time soon.

I guess everybody isn't suited for stream fishing.

Chicken Coop - 4   Trevor - 0

Enchanted Valley

We were small standing there, on the edge of a high mountain meadow in Southern Utah; the middle of nowhere. The gentle valley was rimmed with Aspen aglow in late summer warm yellow. It was still, so very still, not a wisp of wind to ruffle the Aspen leaves.

"Listen," Fran whispered, "you can hear the quiet."

"Ya, right," I said, nodding agreement. My wife has always been sensitive to subtleties of nature. The silence was eerie, not a bird, bug, or critter disturbed the solitude. Then Darin, our ten-year-old, and Billy, his sidekick-shadow, who lives down the street, finally piled out of the car. They had been giggling like girls for the better part of the last hour. Apparently they weren't done yet.

There was a woman in the restaurant where we had breakfast whose butt cheeks stuck out, actually hung down, from her all-too-short frayed blue jean shorts. My guess is those elongated blotchy buns were just obscene enough to get them going. It wasn't a pretty sight.

"I don't see any stream," Darin grumbled.

"We pasted over a culvert back there," I said, pointing to the lowest point on the grassy road we came in on, I didn't actually see any water. "Come on, kids, let's walk down and check it out."

The manager of the condo we'd rented at Brian Head, Utah, gave us directions to a remote meadow where, he claimed, the original movie version of *The Last of the Mohicans* was shot in 1936 – the one where Randolph Scott played Hawkeye.

Billy asked, "What's *The Last of the Mohicans* anyway?"

"I didn't know you were a history buff, Billy."

"Huh?"

"It was a story written by one of America's earliest authors, a guy called *James Fennimore Cooper*. His book was about the French and Indian war."

"A huh," Billy grunted just like he was interested.

"Two of his characters, Hawkeye and a Mohican Indian called Chingachgook fought right here in this valley."

"I don't see any signs of Indians or a stream," Billy giggled.

I didn't bother to tell him the actual war was fought in the northeast or that the English were involved. I was already in too deep. And . . . the boys were still into the elongated butt cheeks.

The guy managing the condo, told us the creek that ran through the valley had a Brook Trout behind every rock. I was more skeptical than the kids since I couldn't see enough water in that valley to fill a shot-glass.

"Come on Boys, let's check it out."

"Check what out," Darin said with a questioning smirk that teenagers develop to cover their naivety, especially when delivering a smartass remark.

Billy giggled in support. I ignored it as usual.

Where the valley wasn't wooded with Aspen, it was covered with tiny wild flowers and a short bluish-green grass that held tight to the morning dew. The four of us trudged down to the lowest part of this gentle valley. The boys and I with our fly rods, and Fran with a half-read Danielle Steel.

To my surprise the stream, although shallow, was a pretty little thing. It ran clear and cold with twists and turns, gentle runs, and sharp drops with pools at the bottom.

"Spread out, Boys. Try to stay back from the water."

"Hey wait a second, how can I fish and stay away from the water at the same time?" Billy was suddenly alert.

"Sorry, Billy, I forgot you're a newbie. Your best chance to catch the smarter bigger fish is to place your fly without the fish realizing you are there."

"Can't the fish see us?"

"Not necessarily, Billy. All fish point into the current and, just like us, they don't have eyes in the back of their heads."

"So?"

"So you can stay behind them if you move upstream and only land your fly in front of wherever you think they might be hiding."

"Can you show us?"

"Okay." I walked a few feet toward the creek, crouched down and duck-walked a few more steps toward the water, then, got on my hands and knees to get even lower. When I was close enough, I dropped the fly over a grass overhang half way through bend. Almost instantly, a seven-inch Brookie took my fly downstream before I could set the hook. I let him challenge me for a minute or two then gently lifted him out at the end of the bend.

I looked at Billy, smiled, and said. "Do that. When you catch enough for your supper, five or six, we'll go back to the condo and cook 'em and eat 'em."

Billy said, "Aren't we gonna' cast?"

"Cast if you like, but remember you can only eat what you catch."

"Okay," Billy said. Darin just smiled.

"And boys, don't keep anything smaller than the one we just caught. Okay?"

They shook their heads. I hiked far enough downstream to give the kids some space. I had already seen enough to know there were too many fish with little food, and I was pretty sure under-fed Brookies would hit just about anything. Each of our rods had a strong leader with a little soft hackle brown, gray, or black bivisibles tied on the end. We each carried a box with a few flies but the selection was limited. I figured no matter what they chose to fish with or how skilled their technique, the boys would catch a lot of very small fish before they had five big enough to eat.

After four days of togetherness, Fran was into a book,

the boys were heading in the opposite direction, and I was alone. So small, so very small, I felt standing in this mountain paradise. I stood there for the longest time trying to commit the serene splendor to memory. A frog jumped breaking my trance. *I'm not gonna' hurt you, little one.* I thought. *Okay, time to go fishin'.* I studied the stream, evaluated my choices, and starting to fish, I quickly became part of the valley.

Three hours passed in a few precious moments. I wasn't done yet, but, the time was agreed upon before we started. I was surprised to see the boys were fishing separately. *Way to go boys.*

"Darin, Billy," I shouted, "come on in."

The kids were excited and happy. I enjoyed their success. We cleaned twenty-one fish kneeling next to the stream. The biggest one was about eight inches and the smallest was too small to be legal. We kept it any way. The deep crimson red flesh color seemed darker than any I'd ever seen before.

Potato chips, baked beans, and mountain top Brookies; what a great fish fry, the best any of us could ever remember. Or probably ever will.

Even without the Indians, it was an enchanted day in the valley.

A lot of small can be really big.
Ruby Sue Tootser

"I hear babies cryin'. I watch them grow.
They'll learn much more than I'll ever know
And I think to myself
What a wonderful world"

- Weiss and Thiele, made famous by Loui Armstrong

It's called Fishing, not Catching

I dragged my tired butt into the kitchen after a long day on the stream and plopped down in a chair across from Amy, my six year old granddaughter. The only fish I'd managed to fool was clever enough to take me into the branches of a downed tree before I could turn him. Today was his day; tomorrow who knows.

"How many fish, Grandpa?" Amy asked enthusiastically.

"I was skunked, Sweetheart."

"Skunked? You mean no fish," Amy said with her little impish smile.

"That's what it means alright."

"Too bad, Grandpa, you must-of had a bad day."

Her statement took me aback and I paused to think for a moment. "No Sweetie, I had a great day."

"You did? It was fun to get skunked?"

"I usually enjoy fishing, whether I catch fish or not."

Her lips scrunched to the side of her face and with her eyes peering at me from the top of the sockets, she said. "You were gone almost all day, you seem really tired, you got skunked, but you still had a great day?"

"Right, Amy, I didn't catch any fish, but still had a wonderful day."

"How can that be any fun Grandpa? You didn't get nothin'."

They call it fishing, Sweetheart, not catching.

"Huh?"

"It fun, Amy, because sometime it's fun to try as hard as you can even if you get skunked." I hoped that would close the conversation.

"You sure you had a good day, Grandpa?"

"I did," I said, starting to doubt myself. "Trout are very smart and hard to catch. It's the challenge that makes it fun. Sort of a game between you and the fish.

"Can you teach me how to be a trout fisherman, Grandpa"

Whenever a sibling shows the slightest interest in anything grandparents do, most of us will jump at the chance to encourage them. "I'd be happy too, Sweetheart. When you get a little older I will teach you to cast a fly, show you the basics, but a lot of what you need to know you will learn on your own." I knew the moment I said "learn on your own" that I was in too deep.

"Why's that?"

"You will need to learn to think like a fish and that can't be taught."

"How do I learn to do that then?" The smirk was back on her face.

I realized she didn't have a clue what I was talking about. "Thinking like a fish means knowing their habits. That's the challenge that separates good trout fishermen from just fisherman."

"Do you think like a fish grandpa?"

"I try, Sweetheart, but I have to admit, just when I think I've figured them out, the trout must figure me out – they can be too smart for me."

"Like today, Grandpa."

"Exactly like today, Sweetie."

"You might want to look for another hobby, Grandpa."

"Thank you, Amy. I'll think about it."

The Legend of Frank Soul

Twenty-year-old Frank Soul enlisted in the Army on December 27, 1941, and spent four and a half years marching across Africa and most of Europe. When the war ended, he landed in Wisconsin where he inherited a small farm from a recluse uncle that he met only once as a small boy.

War-weary and a loner by nature, Frank seemed almost as aloof as his uncle had been. He kept to himself, friendly, but distant enough to interest the ever-curious local busybodies. Frank didn't work the land or have a job, but he always seemed to have money for his basic needs; gas, groceries, and a beer or two at the local watering hole, a drab "shot and a beer" joint called, *The Club Tavern*. The quiet man's source of income was a mystery that fed the gossip.

Some say the legend actually started when Frank got an official USGA topographic map of the county. The Club bartender claimed. "One of the local fisherman told Frank about a secret trout spot over a couple of beers." As the story goes, there's a legendary fishing hole on one of our streams that locals call, "God's hole." No one is quite sure just where it is but, they say anyone, even a ghost, can catch a creel of nice Brown Trout there. No one really knew exactly when it took place or how it happened. But it did.

Actually the speculators were right on.

I first learned about "God's hole" from an old timer who claimed to have spent most of his sober moments on streams all over the area. And, yes I used the cartographic knowledge I learned in the Army to pinpoint the exact spot, using an old pen-and-ink photocopy of a USGS topographic map of the area. It detailed the terrain rather well, including elevations.

It was a cool June morning in 1947. I was miles down the road when a hint of daybreak was a soft orange glow on the southeast horizon. The forlorn wail of a loon signaled that I wasn't the only one feeling desolate. Tops of scrub pines peeked through misty fog that hovered over the lowlands, and the silent Northwood's dawn became a mystical world that demanded my reverence. *Look, listen,* I said to myself. *Thank you, God, for a chance to be part of it.*

I turned east off Highway 52 north of town onto a dirt road that became more path than road with each mile I covered. Knowing full well that the branches would put a few more scratches on *Baby*, my already well marked Ford pick-em-up truck, I asked her to go into places where tanks would avoid. *Come on, Baby,* I said, as the road turned into a path that looked like it had been made by animals rather than man. It ended at a little ridge with swamp land on three sides.

I reached into the truck bed, grabbed my rod, old jacket, net, and stepped into leaky old waders and into a world where outside anxiety was replaced with meaningless challenges that only involved me and a few very crafty fish. The memories of war never could penetrate leaky boots.

My pulse thumped like a tom-tom as I unfolded the topographic map I'd studied for hours the night before. *Okay,* I said to myself, *let's get it on.* According to my calculations the stream was about three quarters of a mile due East. The topographic map told me I was in for a trudge through wet lowland, but the brushy swamp wasn't as bad as I anticipated. We had a few months of drought; I guess that had dried up some of the muck.

I came upon the stream in half the time I'd allotted. *The beginning of another Grand Canyon,* I thought, surprised to find the stream about ten feet lower than the brushy bank I was standing on. When I slowly peeked over the edge, I was pleased to see what looked like at a rocky bottom and deep dark pools of crystal clear water. Flowing between boulders and ancient logs, the creek twisted and turned to create nature's soothing sound unique to meandering trout streams. I love that sound.

A flash of golden color caught my eye at the surface of the pool just upstream. *Too big to be a chub,* I thought. *This may be my day.* I quietly walked the bank downstream about twenty yards, got on my hands and knees, crawled backward a few feet, and eased myself over the edge. The toes of my boots caught the incline and, with a long step down I was in the water. *So far, so good.* Ever so slowly I worked my way back up stream to a spot where I could put a dry-fly in the run at the head of the pool.

The fish flashed again, *whoa, now that's a grand-daddy if I ever saw one. Take your time,* I said to myself; *one of the harder things I try to do.*

The nameless fly at the end of my leader was a small number 14 gray bivisible. *Thank you, Jesus,* I said to myself as I "false-cast" enough line to reach the spot I'd chosen for the fly to drop. *"Perfect,"* I thought as it landed in the current and move downstream faster than I was gathering line. I could see the fish hit. My line went rigid in an instant, and I knew he had hooked himself in spite of my inept line stripping. *"Thank you."*

After several attempts to escape – taking runs up and downstream, a very respectable, fourteen inch brown flopped in my net. I took two more browns from that pretty little stretch before I realized I'd overstayed my welcome.

The sun was 10 o'clock high and it was warming fast. *"Upstream or down, Hmm,* I thought. Downstream looked like pretty slow water; *upstream it is then.* With the pressure of the current, stronger than it appeared, I carefully planted each foot on the unfamiliar bottom. When I reached the spot where I hooked the first trout and looked it over carefully. A quick drop into a deep pool. *Trout haven if I'd ever saw on.*

Above my new favorite hole I found a long, very slow looking run for about quarter of a mile. Decision time. *I'll go a ways to see around the bend.* Wrong choice.

I had only gone about fifty feet when I could feel my boots being sucked into the muck that had replaced the sandy rocky bottom. I pulled my right leg with all my might, but I couldn't get it to release from the bottom's grip. I tried the left leg with the same result.

I just stood there for a few moments thinking, *Okay Dumbo, what now?* It felt like I was slowly sinking deeper into the water but I wasn't sure. *If I can reach the bank maybe I can pull myself out.* I tried to touch it with my rod tip hoping to snag a root, but it was just out of reach.

I could use a little help here, God. No answer. I vaguely recalled a bit of woodsy wisdom that suggested laying horizontal, letting your waders fill with water. The buoyancy was supposed to help release your boots from the muck. *What the hell, at this stage, I'll try anything. Here goes.* I stretched forward with my arms extended until my face touched the water. My boots filled with water. *Damn that's cold.* I held that position for several minutes, all the while trying to wiggle my right boot free. *Stupid, stupid, stupid.* This was not going to work.

"A fine mess you've got us into, Ollie," My self-indulgent humor didn't help. I was "SOL." The first wave of panic washed over me. *What now? Think, think, think, man.*

I pulled the wader straps off my shoulders and pushed them down into the water, all the way to my knees which happened to be where the muck began. I pulled one leg as hard as I could. No luck. "Help, help," I shouted knowing full well nobody lived within miles of where I was stranded. *How long can I stand there? Nobody has a clue where I am. I wish I wasn't such a loner.* Minutes felt like hours. Reality can be a scary state. *Try something, anything.*

I snipped the fly off with a nail clippers, reeled in the line, took the reel off my over-priced rod and slipped it into the creel. I pulled the rod apart and slipped connector end of the stiff section down my boot along side my foot until it came to a stop. Water filled the boot around my foot and the suction dissipated. I pushed the boot bottom down with the rod and pulled my foot upward. *Whoa, this is gonna work.* Relief turned to elation as I felt my foot clear the boot. *Thank you, thank you, Jesus.* Having one foot on the boot instead of in it was like freedom from shackles.

As I tried to create some leverage, my free foot and the boot sank even deeper into the heavy muck. The muck seemed to be holding my leg without the boot. Hours passed, night came slowly, I couldn't stop it.

I realized this was not going to end well and began my conversation with God.

106

Several weeks passed before a game warden became suspicious of the old pickup and the possibility of a poacher trapping muskrats in the posted wetlands. He followed the faint tracks into the swamp all the way to the stream. *Yep poachers,* he thought just before he spotted Frank, bent at the hip, face down just under the water.

It took four men in a John boat with two ropes to pull him free of the gripping muck. He came out without his waders. As far as anyone knows they are still down there. Three stiff Brown Trout that any trout fisherman would be proud of were in his creel.

More local people than Frank ever met attended the funeral, and everyone in town became experts as *"The Legend of Frank Soul"* evolved.

You can find Frank Soul's headstone up at
Whispering Hills.

Frank Soul
July 4, 1920 – June 21, 1948
Died with his waders on
3 Browns in his creel

The Fisherman

Huffing and puffing like a big bad wolf I managed to crawl over the last monster boulder around a shaggy white pine to the top of the hill. *Whoo, whoo, whoa,* with couple extra breaths, I said to myself, "No doubt about it, I'm not the man I used to be." Hell, I wasn't the man I was before I climbed the hill.

I slipped the tattered leather creel strap over my head and unbuttoned my canvas hunting jacket. I'd worn that old jacket on hot and cold days alike for as long as I could remember. It was part of me as a trout fisherman and . . . I had it in my head that the jacket was lucky. Why? I have no idea. Many a time I've been skunked wearing it.

My saturated tee shirt clung to my back like extra skin. It was a cold, clammy sweat, probably my morning coffee not making it all the way through my system. My waders didn't leak but still felt damp inside. I stood up and pulled them down below my waist. You probably guessed what came next and don't need a description. However, I did feel better.

I plopped my achy bones down on an inviting blanket of grass next to a fallen pine; the perfect backrest. I grabbed a Miller Lite, one of three that was tucked in my wicker creel along with my usual assortment of seldom used stuff, all too important to leave behind. I popped the can lid, leaned back and closed my eyes. *I'll rest here for just a minute or two.*

I woke up a half hour later with a dry mouth and the beer can still in my hand. What luck, I mused, taking a swig. I thanked the Lord for providing a cool day. "Not all that warm," I said, taking another gulp and saluting Him with a tip of the can.

The stream at the bottom of the hill was a beautiful sight to wake up to. Sparkling clear water sliding over little rock dams, rambling, rushing, dropping from one level to the next, creating pool after pool on its way to the ocean. I wonder if God was giving me a peek at heaven when He created trout streams.

I sensed more than saw something move downstream. A squirrel, deer or raccoon was my guess. I peered in the direction of the movement hoping to see the critter, proving to myself that I belonged out here in the wild. Nothing doing, I just wasn't wild enough to really know what went on around me.

Suddenly I realized a fisherman had edged around the bend and was standing in plain view at the shallow side of the stream. He seemed to belong there, a natural part of the environment. How did he move that far without my noticing? And, damned if Mr. Stealth wasn't going to plow right through the stretch of water I'd hiked my butt off to fish.

The guy stood motionless in the shallows for the longest time. *What's his problem,* I wondered. When I saw his head move ever so slightly, I realized he was surveying the water, carefully studying each section of the stream. He wasn't a big man, maybe a couple of inches taller than me, although it was hard to tell with him in waders. I guessed he was about twenty pounds lighter than I am and probably 30 years younger.

He took a wide path, moving deliberately without causing a ripple in the water. Eventually he arrived at the spot he was headed for. *Not too bad,* I thought. That's the same section of stream I always fish. *Mr. Stealth has done this a time or two.*

His cast was more sidearm than text book, but a natural rhythm and perfectly timed. The fly landed on the water as if it were dropped into the perfect spot by the hand of God. I couldn't believe the effort didn't entice a fish, but it didn't seem to bother Mr. Stealth. He just paused for what seemed to be longer than my patience would have dictated and repeated the process. As the fly descended about two feet upstream from the first cast, the water exploded before it even landed on the water; like the trout was waiting for another chance. The fish looked to be about 14 inches, not huge, but I was impressed.

The fisherman was in no hurry to land his prize.

Holding the line taut, he let the fish run upstream and down several times only nudging him in once the trout lost the fight. As if choreographed he pulled a worn wooden net from his hip, swooped down and picked up the fish in one fluid motion. A moment later he stuck the trout through the hole in the lid of a wicker creel that looked smaller than the fish was long. I couldn't help but be a bit jealous; the fisherman seemed to do everything I would have done only with more patience than I can remember ever having.

Instead of going back to the same spot, hoping to meet the fish's big brother like I would've done, Mr. Smooth moved upstream into, what I considered the best position to attack my favorite stretch; a place where the stream narrowed as it squeezed between two large boulders forming a deep run that evolved into an even deeper pool at the bottom.

The tight little opening at the head of the run was protected by a low hanging bough of a shaggy white pine. Over the years those guard dog branches caught more of my flies than I caught fish; I love that spot.

After a couple air casts the fisherman leaned forward releasing the line. The fly gently landed on the very tip of the lowest branch. *Oops, missed by an inch. This Isaac Walton is human after all.* He didn't bother with fancy snaps or pull-release routines to try to break the tree's grasp on the fly. He just grabbed the line and pulled until the leader broke. *A man after my own heart*, I thought. I'd often spent way too much time trying to save a fly when I had several duplicates it in my fly box.

He took his sweet time tying another fly to the leader, then gave the fly a jerk double-checking his efforts. After flogging the air again, his next cast landed about 4 feet left of the headwater. *There's nothing there, buddy,* I thought, but a few moments after the fly hit the water, the fisherman flipped the trickiest little roll-cast I'd ever seen. The fly landed smack-dab in the middle of the little opening I'd unsuccessfully tried to reach more often than I'd admit, even to myself.

By the time the fly reached the bottom of the run I figured, *oh well, perfection has never been a guarantee of success*; trout are seldom impressed with man's imitation bugs. I knew I was wrong the moment he raised the old bamboo rod holding it close to his forehead. The rod bent to the max and the leader cut through the strong current like its force was irrelevant. I saw the golden flash of a mature Brown and knew immediately the angler had a worthy opponent.

He seemed to sense the fish charging upstream was not about to allow his enemy to turn him. When I saw the fisherman move in order to keep up with the Brown, I knew he was in trouble. The drop-off in front of him was lined with slippery rocks; I could hardly bring myself to watch, and I was too far away to warn him.

He took a step forward, another, one more . . . his feet went out from under him. After sliding into the water he ended up on his seat with water spilling over the lip of his waders. Throughout the ordeal, he held his rod high keeping the line tension steady enough to keep fish from his escape. The fisherman managed to get up and continue moving forward, still in total control. Before long he swooped up the fish with the same rhythm as his first catch. I guessed getting a wet butt was an everyday occurrence with Mr. Not-So-Smooth.

Once the Brown was safely tucked away in his basket, the fisherman worked his way to the bank and crawled over the boulders onto a patch of short grassy weeds. He pushed and pulled until he managed to get out of his waders. Not all that easy because the water creates a suction. Been there, done that – all too often. As he dumped the water out, I noticed he was wearing a hunting jacket. *Son-of-a-gun, I thought I was the only one who fished in a jacket like that.* His was too new for my liking, but it was nice to see someone in his generation that liked the same garb as me.

It didn't take the fisherman long before he was back in the water unknowingly showing off his methodical attack on my favorite stretch of stream. Like a general analyzing the battlefield, the fisherman conquered each obstacle by studying the water, creating a plan of attack and executing it with the precision of a sharpshooter.

I watched with admiration. The fisherman moved effortlessly picking and choosing only the likeliest spots to fish. He always landed the fly where he wanted without causing a splash or disturbing the water. He was very much the fisherman I'd always strived to be.

Trout fishing is anything but a group sport, and I knew the fisherman wouldn't appreciate the interruption, but I had to tell this guy how much I enjoyed watching him perform his magic.

I pulled up my waders, slipped the creel harness over my head, picked up my rod and headed directly toward the spot where I would intersect with the fisherman. The hill seemed steeper than usual as I half-slid, half-stumbled, grabbing branches along the way. Gravity sent me to the bottom sooner than I planned.

After going around one more pine, my boots hit the pebbles at the edge of the water. I looked up expecting to startle the angler in front of me. He wasn't there.

I looked upstream and down. There was no way anyone could have got out of the stream faster than I crashed my way down the hill. Even if he did manage to get out that quickly, he should be standing next to me.

Where did he go? He couldn't vanish. Did I imagine it all . . . or was he a dream, a ghost of my younger-self, the way I wished I was?

Go Fish